"... AN EXTRAORDINARY BLEND OF PASSION AND DIGNITY ... guides us deep into the blazing quiet of our own being, where prayer becomes the magic carpet that carries us to union with the object of our most profound longing—a union that results in the melting of lover into Beloved, so that only love remains. This, Llewellyn teaches us, is our sacred birthright."

— MIRABAI STARR, translator, *Dark Night of the Soul*
by St. John of the Cross, and *The Interior Castle*
and *The Book of My Life* by St. Teresa of Avila

"THIS IS A PRECIOUS LITTLE BOOK ... one of those rare works that emerges from the heart and leads us into unified consciousness. Its gentle and poetic words echo the calling of my heart—reminding me to return home."

— EDWARD BASTIAN, PH.D.,
Spiritual Paths Foundation

"... A WISE BOOK ON PRAYER ... expresses the vibrant possibilities of our inter-spiritual age. Standing rooted in his own Sufi tradition, Vaughan-Lee brings forth essential teachings on Christian prayer which lead to a more profound understanding of Sufi mysticism. Highly recommended spiritual reading!"

— DAVID FRENETTE, author of
The Path of Centering Prayer:
Deepening Your Experience of God

D0121987

PRAYER
of the HEART
in
Christian & Sufi Mysticism

LLEWELLYN VAUGHAN-LEE

PRAYER *of the* HEART
in Christian & Sufi Mysticism

First published in the United States in 2012 by
The Golden Sufi Center
P.O. Box 456, Point Reyes, California 94956
www.goldensufi.org

ISBN 13: 978-1-890350-35-2
ISBN 10: 1-890350-35-4

Printed and Bound by Thompson-Shore, Inc.

Library of Congress Cataloging-in-Publication Data

Vaughan-Lee, Llewellyn.
  The prayer of the heart in Christian & Sufi mysticism / by
Llewellyn Vaughan-Lee.
     p. cm.
  Includes bibliographical references (p.) and index.
  ISBN 978-1-890350-35-2 (pbk. : alk. paper)
1. Contemplation--Comparative studies. 2. Prayer--Christianity--
Comparative studies. 3. Prayer--Sufism--Comparative studies.
4. Jesus prayer. 5. Sufi chants. I. Title.
  BV5091.C7V38 2012
  297.4'382--dc23
                              2011041192

CONTENTS

THE LADDER OF DIVINE GRACES[1]

which experience has made known
to those inspired by God

The first step is that of purest prayer.
From this there comes a warmth of heart,
And then a strange, a holy energy,
Then tears wrung from the heart, God-given.
Then peace from thoughts of every kind.
From this arises purging of the intellect,
And next the vision of heavenly mysteries.
Unheard-of light is born from this ineffably,
And thence, beyond all telling,
the heart's illumination.
Last comes—a step that has no limit
Though compassed in a single line—
Perfection that is endless.

God Most High hath brought forth creation and said,
"Entrust Me with your secrets.
If you do not do this, then look toward Me.
If you do not do this, then listen to Me.
If you do not do this, then wait at My door.
If you do none of this,
tell Me of your needs."

SAHL[2]

PREFACE

God, the Great Beloved, is neither masculine nor feminine. As much as It has a divine masculine side, so It has an awe-inspiring feminine aspect. However, at times in this book God is referred to as masculine, He. This is for the sake of consistency. The Christian mystical writings of St. Teresa of Avila, as well as the Sufi authors who are quoted, refer to God as He.

FOREWORD

It is widely known that during the final decade of his life Thomas Merton, that great contemporary Christian mystic, was deeply drawn to Buddhism. What is less widely known is that he was equally and in some ways even more intensely drawn to Sufism. Somewhere during those years he had happened upon Louis Massignon's French commentary of a treatise on the heart by al-Hallāj, a ninth-century Sufi saint. Clearly galvanized by what he found here, Merton referred to this text again and again, both in his formal writings and in his journals. In particular, Massignon's explication of the *point vierge*, that mysterious divine ground at the very center of the human heart (known by Sufis as the *sirr*, or secret), furnished the impetus for Merton's stirring final paragraph in his essay "A Member of the Human Race":

Then it was as if I suddenly saw the secret beauty of their hearts, the depths of their hearts where neither sin nor desire nor self-knowledge can reach, the core of their reality ...

Again that expression, *le point vierge* (I cannot translate it) comes in here. At the center of our being is a point of nothingness which is untouched by sin and illusion, a point of pure truth, a point or spark which belongs only to God, which is never at our disposal, from which God disposes of our lives, which is inaccessible to the fantasies of our own mind or the brutalities of our own will. This little point of nothingness and of absolute poverty is the pure glory of God written within us, as our poverty, as our indigence, as our sonship. It is like a pure diamond blazing with the invisible light of heaven. It is in everybody, and if we could only see it, we would see these billions of points of light coming together in the face and blaze of a sun that would make all the darkness and cruelty of life vanish completely.

In the mirror of Sufism Merton came to recognize his own Christian heart deeply illumined.

Sufism and Christianity are joined at the heart; of that there can be little doubt. I have come to that conclusion in my own right, in the course of my own twenty-year quest to recover Christianity's authentic Wisdom tradition. Along the course of this journey I have received nurturance from many Sufi teachers, Llewellyn Vaughan-Lee being first among them. These wonderful mentors have helped me to reclaim the great path of love at the heart of my own Christian tradition: indelibly present though often veiled in the theologically abstruse language in which Christianity so quickly became accustomed to presenting itself. In my mind's eye I often imagine a kind of hand-off, which may be both historically and politically incorrect but continues to ring with an inner truth: that as institutional Christianity became increasingly dogmatic and propositional in its for-mulations in those centuries following its elevation to the official religion of the Roman Empire, Sufism arose in the cradle of Islam to receive and nurture those teachings on the heart that had first been planted in those near-eastern lands directly from the living heart of Jesus.

Sufism and Christianity are joined at the heart—perhaps literally, and certainly spiritually and symbolically. They are kindred pathways of transfiguration through love. Both traditions picture the spiritual journey with the same core metaphor: as a cosmic love song that begins in exile and ends in divine intimacy. From the soul-wrenching cry of Rūmī's reed flute to the profound theological metaphors of Teresa of Avila's interior mansions and Julian of Norwich's hazelnut; from *The Conference of the Birds* to *The Cloud of Unknowing*, both traditions acknowledge the anguish of separation while radiating the assurance of ecstatic reunion when that which had been misperceived as two is recognized as sublimely One. As my own teacher, Father Thomas Keating, puts it: "The notion that God is absent is the fundamental illusion of the human condition."

Prayer is the pathway toward exposing that illusion and is itself a direct gateway into what another of my esteemed Sufi mentors, Kabir Helminski, calls "the great electro-magnetic field of love." In the teachings of the Christian East on Prayer of the Heart and in the foundational Sufi practice of *dhikr*, the ecstatic devotion arising out of the fully-embodied recitation of the names of God, we find a common pathway of prayer that overcomes egoic self-ishness and drama and ultimately catapults us into the blue of the flame of pure self-oblation, where miraculously we are not destroyed but rather birthed into true personhood. With the understated simplicity of a true spiritual master, Llewellyn Vaughan-Lee seamlessly weaves these comple-mentary traditions into a single tapestry of singular power and beauty. Pay particular attention to the things he has to say about breath; if you find them as astonishing as I did, you will sense yet again what gifts Sufism may have to offer to a Christianity struggling to reawaken to its ancient understandings of the crucial role of embodiment in prayer. A renewed appreciation for embodiment, particularly as carried in the breath, the missing link that releases us from those endless tedious discussions about whether prayer (understood as verbal petition) "works" and instead plunges us into the dynamic ground of that "great electro-magnetic field," where our absence has been noticed and is sorely missed.

I began these introductory remarks by citing Merton's haunting vision of "these billions of points of light coming together in the face and blaze of a sun that would make all the darkness and cruelty of life vanish forever." Not surprisingly, given that they have been feasting by those same Sufi streams, Llewellyn Vaughan-Lee offers a nearly identical image in one of his earliest books, *The Bond with The Beloved* (1993). The following paragraph on page 26, underlined and starred in my well-thumbed edition, was what first ignited my connection with Sufism and my reconnection with a nearly abandoned inner conviction that prayer was utterly real and utterly needed, not just for personal healing and "self-realization" but for the very life of our planet:

As we silently work upon ourselves, the energy of our devotion becomes a point of light within the world. At the present time a map is being unfolded made of the lights of the lovers of God. The purpose of this map is to change the inner energy structure of the planet. In previous ages this energy structure was held by sacred places, stone circles, temples, and cathedrals. In the next stage of our collective evolution it is the hearts of individuals who will hold the cosmic note of the planet. This note can be recognized as a song of joy being born within the hearts of seekers. It is a quality of joy that is being infused into the world. It is the heartbeat of the world and needs to be heard in our cities and towns.

With this most recent book, Llewellyn Vaughan-Lee offers yet another profound contribution to the "collective evolution of our hearts," and it is with joy, indeed, that I receive it.

—*The Rev. Cynthia Bourgeault*
Eagle Island, Maine
September 2011

INTRODUCTION

At the heart of most religions is prayer: a way to communicate with God. It can take the form of prescribed prayers, the rituals of inner communion. But it can also take the form of personal prayer, in which we find our own way of being with God, with the Divine that is the source of everything.[3] And for the mystic the deepest form of personal prayer is the prayer of the heart, in which we are drawn within our own heart where we are able to be alone with our Beloved. Here our heart cries out to God, and here we also rest in silence—waiting, listening, merging into love. The prayer of the heart can be found within both the Christian and Sufi mystical traditions.

This small book is drawn from my own experiences of the prayer of the heart as I have travelled along the Sufi path of love for almost forty years. My understanding of this inner prayer within the Christian mystical tradition comes mainly from the writings of St. Teresa of Avila. St. Teresa describes her own deep experiences of mystical prayer in both *Interior Castle* and her autobiography, *The Life of St. Teresa of Jesus*. Despite the difficulties of following mystical practices under the watchful eye of the Inquisition, she was drawn beyond the mental repetition of prescribed prayers, into the silence of the heart's prayer, where she experienced her own mystic communion with the Divine. In *Interior Castle* she describes seven different "mansions" of the soul and the progress by which prayer and spiritual practice take us into the innermost place of mystical marriage of the soul with God. In *The Life of St. Teresa of Jesus* she outlines different degrees of prayer that belong to this deepening relationship with the Divine.

The passion and intensity of St. Teresa's inner life of prayer have always given me a deep source of joy, as I found within the Christian mystical tradition a description of mystical prayer that resonated so much with my own experience within the Sufi tradition. She writes of being taken by prayer, absorbed, merged into the divine mystery within the heart, in ways that speak to the single source of love to which all mystics are drawn. And while the monastic tradition to which St. Teresa belonged is externally very different from the Sufi path, which is lived in the midst of worldly life, of family, work, and all our other activities, she has a very grounded mysticism that balanced her inner visions and intense states of rapture. For her "God lives among the pots and pans,"[4] and her simple enjoyment of food is echoed in her saying, "When praying, pray, when eating porridge, eat porridge."[5]

Although St. Teresa continually refers to herself as lacking in learning, she describes with detail and precision as well as passion the different stages of prayer. From her own experience she guides us through the deepening communion of silence with the Divine which finally overwhelms us with its presence: how the receptive soul is taken into rapture, merged into union. Reading her experiences I was deeply moved to discover how they correspond with the Sufi stages of deepening absorption within the heart that take us to oneness with our Beloved.

In each path we find the simple prayer of the heart in which the practitioner leaves behind the mind and its thoughts. Rather than engaging in any active process of prayer or meditation, we simply go within the heart, that spiritual center of our being. To quote St. Theophan the Recluse:

> The concentration
> of attention in the heart—
> this is the starting point of prayer.[6]

Just as the physical heart is the center of our material body, so the spiritual heart is the center of our spiritual body, the organ of our divine consciousness. It is within the heart that we can have a direct relationship with God. It is here that divine communion takes place, where we meet our Beloved. The French Benedictine, Henri Lassaux, beautifully describes this quality of the heart in his book on prayer: "The heart is the place of our origin in which the soul is, as it were, coming from the hands of God and waking up to itself."[7] And just as St. Teresa discusses the different, more and more inward mansions of the soul, so have Sufi mystics described the different chambers of the heart that lead us deeper and deeper, into the core of our being where we are always one with God.[8]

To begin the practice of the prayer of the heart one needs to be alone, to allow oneself to descend from the mind into the heart. It is the feeling quality of the heart that draws us back to God.[9] This feeling may be love, longing, sadness— however it is that our heart expresses itself. It might be no particular feeling, but simply a quality of stillness or silence. Or it can be just a desire to be alone with God. The heart is a sacred space where we can come to be with our Beloved, so one needs an attitude of receptivity, a feminine quality that eventually becomes a state of surrender to God. In this sacred space we may speak our words of longing, of need, or our words of love. We may pray for our self, for others, for the whole world. We may offer praise or thanks.

Going into the heart we also need to learn to listen. Prayer is a state of inner listening in which we ask to "open our hearts that we may hear Thy voice that constantly cometh from within." If we are attentive, if we learn to wait, we may hear a still, small voice within the heart that is our Beloved speaking to us. The Beloved speaks in whatever way we are uniquely able to hear. His messages of love, as St. Teresa says, are "written very lovingly in such a way that He would have you alone be able to understand what He has written and what He is asking of you in it."[10]

The Christian Orthodox tradition also has a prayer of the heart, the Jesus Prayer, a very simple prayer that brings the mind into the heart. I have included a chapter on it as well. The Jesus prayer is similar to the Sufi practice of the *dhikr*, the remembrance of God through the repetition of a sacred word or phrase. In both the Jesus Prayer and the *dhikr*, the repetition of sacred words strengthens our remembrance of God and helps to awaken the Divine within our heart.

In whatever way we are called to pray, as our prayers deepen we find our self drawn beyond any words into the interior silence of real communion with God. There, in the silence within the heart, a meeting and merging take place that carry us beyond our self into the mystery of divine presence, into the secret nature of love's oneness. Sufi and Christian mystics have mapped out the stages of this journey into love, the way by which, within our own heart and soul, the Beloved is born and then reveals to us the deepest wonder and ecstasy that are within us. But it is for each of us to make our own way along this ancient path, to discover this love, to be in this place of prayer. This little book is just an offering of the heart that brings together these two mystical traditions in the oneness of love to which they belong.

1

PRAYER *and* LISTENING

Inner Receptivity

Prayer is born from need. We feel alone and in need. And only the Divine can answer this need. This need draws us to the place of prayer within us, to our heart that looks towards God.

Calling out from the depths of our being, we make known our need to our self and to God. We pray according to our need, and according to the need of the moment. At different times our needs are different. We may pray for forgiveness, for understanding, for kindness. We may pray that our relationships not be clouded in mistrust or that our children not suffer. All of the myriad difficulties that we encounter in our daily life we can embrace in our prayer, the difficulties of our own self and of family and friends, the troubles of the world.[11] We hope to bring God's attention to these problems, so that infinite love and grace can reach into our world and help with the pain of being human.

Prayer is infinitely powerful because it connects us with God's infinite power. Praying, we offer up the difficulties of living in a world in which the Divine often appears to be absent, in the deepest knowledge that only the Divine who is the source of all life and all love can really help us. We who are so small and alone look to God, and so turn our attention from the many back to the One. Sometimes people think, "Why should I bother God? How can my difficulties be of concern to this Great Being?" But this is the voice of the ego, because it sets the individual falsely apart from God. We are a part of God's world, and if we are in need we should turn towards God.

So many times it appears that our prayer is not heard, that we are forgotten, alone. And yet as the mystic says, "If the heart has heard the prayer, God has heard the prayer." And more important than any specific answer is the act itself of prayer, the turning towards God. In our busy lives it is so easy to forget the Divine, to be immersed in our own problems and our own selves. The mystic knows that what really matters is the inner connection of the heart in which our heart opens and cries. It is something so simple and yet so easily overlooked. Prayer is a way to be with God.

We each have our own way of being with this inner-most mystery, our own way of prayer. For some of us prayer takes place in the dark hours of the night, when we lie awake and our need is most pressing. Some find it easiest to pray as they walk, or find the presence of nature a way to gain access to this inner communion. Others may pray while they are in their garden, feeling the presence of the Divine among their flowers. Some pray when they see suffering, while others may find their heart opens when they experience beauty. For the mystic the prayer of the heart draws us deep within the center of our being where we can be alone with our Beloved, where the heart can cry and we can be present with its cry. Where we can speak and live the deepest longing of our soul: to be with God.

Both the Sufi and Christian mystical traditions have cultivated a practice of contemplation that takes us deep into the heart where we can be alone with God. Sufism is a path of love in which the lover is taken by love and longing back to the Beloved, from the experience of separation from God to the state of union within the heart. In Sufism we follow this return to love through the practice of a heart meditation or *murāqaba* in which we put the mind into the heart. Immersing our self in the heart, we allow the energy of love to slow down the mind and its many thoughts, until eventually we arrive at a state of empty receptivity, in which we patiently wait within the heart. Even if thoughts come and go, we do not pay them any attention but remain in this state of empty inner awareness. In this interior place we may come to hear the words of our Beloved, experience divine presence, or merge deeper into the silence that belongs to love.

3

In Christian mysticism the Prayer of Quiet is a practice of being silent and listening to God. In this listening stillness, this inner receptivity, the soul becomes infused with divine presence. St. Teresa of Avila describes how Prayer of Quiet is a spark of the true love of God that makes itself felt as peace and overwhelming joy or bliss. Our faculties are absorbed in God, who works within us. Even speaking [e.g., vocal prayer and meditation] wearies our soul; "it wishes to do nothing but love."[12]

Prayer of Quiet also has similarities with Centering Prayer developed by Father Thomas Keating, which draws the practitioner into a state of receptive stillness, bringing the mind into the heart. In the words of Father Keating, "Silence is the language God speaks."[13] This practice has its seeds in the contemplative prayer of the early Desert Fathers. Centering Prayer often begins with meditating on a word or phrase, while Prayer of Quiet, like the Sufi heart meditation, focuses on silence and inner receptivity.

Learning to pray is learning to listen. Within the heart we learn to wait with patience for God's words, which may come even when we have not asked. Listening itself is a form of prayer, in which our whole being is receptive. Prayer is communion with God; we share with Him our needs, and we also learn to be attentive, as Rūmī so beautifully describes:

Make everything in you an ear, each atom of your being, and you will hear at every moment what the

Source is whispering to you, just to you and for you, without any need for my words or anyone else's. You are—we all are—the beloved of the Beloved, and in every moment, in every event of your life, the Beloved is whispering to you exactly what you need to hear and know. Who can ever explain this miracle? It simply is. Listen and you will discover it every passing moment. Listen, and your whole life will become a conversation in thought and act between you and Him, directly, wordlessly, now and always.[14]

Listening within the heart is attuning our self to our Beloved. We develop the ear of the heart, the inner listening of the soul. Sometimes God communicates directly with words. The Beloved does not often speak in a loud voice, or come banging on the door. Mostly God speaks very quietly, answering our prayers, giving us guidance, or whispering about the secrets of the soul, the mysteries of divine love. We may hear these words as a still, small voice, or a thought suddenly appearing. And our work is to learn to listen, to create an inner space where this voice is not drowned out by the constant chatter of the mind, by anxieties or desires.

In this silence of receptive prayer, the Prayer of Quiet, God can speak directly to the soul. In the words of Miguel de Molinos, one of the defenders of the religious revival of Quietism:

By not speaking nor desiring, and not thinking, she [the contemplative spirit] arrives at the true and perfect mystical silence wherein God speaks with the soul, communicates Himself to it, and in the abyss of its own depths teaches it the most perfect and exalted wisdom. He calls and guides it to this inward solitude and mystical silence, when He says He will speak to it alone in the most secret and hidden part of the heart.[15]

Discrimination

In *Interior Castle* St. Teresa describes in detail "the way in which, when He is pleased to do so, God speaks to the soul."[16] She writes of the different ways God speaks to the soul:

Some of them seem to come from without; others from the innermost depths of the soul; others from the higher part; while others, again, are so completely outside the soul that they can be heard with the ears, and seem to be uttered by a human voice.[17]

She specifically differentiates among three types of divine locution: corporeal, actually heard by the physical powers of hearing; imaginary, heard, but by the faculty of the imagination; and spiritual, without sound but imprinted into the depths of the soul.

But St. Teresa warns about the dangers of being deceived by any voices heard in prayer; they should be treated with caution, even disregarded. If they come from God they will return. But she warns that some words may come from the devil, and she gives helpful guidance as to how to discriminate. She says that "whether they come from within, from above or from without, has nothing to do with their coming from God." Instead, the signs of their divine origin are, first, "the sense of power and authority which they bear with them." Secondly, "that a great tranquility dwells in the soul, which becomes peacefully recollected.... The third sign is that these words do not vanish from the memory for a very long time: some, indeed, never vanish at all."[18]

She also describes other ways in which God speaks to the soul which we can tell to be genuine, rather than either the voice of the devil or our own imagination. The first reason is that "a genuine spiritual voice is so clear that the soul remembers every word."

> The second reason is that … the voice comes unexpectedly … often it refers to things one never thought could happen....
>
> The third reason is that in genuine locutions the soul seems to be hearing something, whereas in locutions invented by the imagination, someone seems to be composing bit by bit what the soul wishes to hear.
>
> The fourth reason is that there is a great difference in the words themselves: in a genuine locution one

single word may contain a world of meaning such as the understanding alone could never put rapidly into human language.

The fifth reason is that … not only can words be heard, but … much more can be understood than the words themselves convey.[19]

All those who learn to listen within know the importance of discrimination: what is the genuine voice of God and what is the voice of the ego, or even split-off parts of our personality or psyche.[20] How easily we are deceived by our mind and ego into imagining what we want to hear, how quickly we are led astray. These guidelines of St. Teresa that come from her own experiences are as valuable today as when they were written centuries ago.

The danger is always that the ego subtly subverts inner listening for its own purposes. The mind and the ego collude to create the voice and the messages that can so easily seduce us; nothing knows our weaknesses better than our own ego. And as we often long for guidance or spiritual reassurance, particularly in our contemporary Western culture that offers so little of either, we need to be careful if the inner voice tells us what we want to hear. In my own experience I have often found the unexpected nature of an answer or inner guidance most clearly points to its being genuine. Because the direction of the answer or the language used is so different to anything I could have thought or imagined, I know that it comes from Another rather than my own mind. It is also a valuable guide to notice if the ego or our personal self has anything to gain from what an inner voice tells us. A real inner voice nourishes the spirit, but rarely our material life or surface self.

One should also always pay attention to the danger of inflation—any sense of being special or any spiritual self-importance developing from what we hear within. We need the wisdom of humility[21] and also the safeguard of common sense. Common sense is a very necessary quality when balancing our inner and outer life. The inner voice may speak to us of the secrets of the soul, but rarely gives us unbalanced advice or instructions.

If we listen with discrimination we find that we are given the wisdom and understanding we need, in ways we do not expect. Sometimes a word, a phrase or a knowing is unexpectedly present within us, in answer to a question asked or unasked, or pointing us in a new or needed direction. In Sufism we may find this knowing "impressed into the heart," as if Another had secretly imprinted it there.

There is also the simple wonder of hearing the words of our Beloved, of knowing that we are not forgotten or alone. Spiritual life is a solitary journey, even in the company of other wayfarers. One can often feel very alone,[22] and it's a deep blessing to hear and know the presence of the One we love. Listening within gives us access to a quality of spiritual companionship that brings infinite wonder. Like *manna* from heaven, it nourishes us in the very center of our being. In the words of St. Teresa,

> Each day the soul wonders more, for she feels that they [the words] have never left her, and perceives quite clearly, in the way that I have described, that they are in the interior of her heart—in the most interior place of all and in its greatest depths. So although, not being a learned person, she cannot say how this is, she feels within her this Divine companionship.[23]

Being Attentive to Love

Prayer is communion with God; we share with our Beloved our needs, and we also learn to be attentive to His words, to His needs for us. And sometimes our Beloved communes with us with images rather than words, speaking with luminous pictures or symbols that speak directly to our soul. These images stay with us long after the time of prayer has passed, and we are drawn to meditate on them over the days and weeks that follow. I have found that such images may be full of meaning that unfolds itself gradually into consciousness, attuning us to the deeper dimension of our own soul and our relationship with God. Some lovers may also hear music or smell fragrances that come from the garden of the heart, and that touch them in unexpected ways.

Or our Beloved may speak to us in dreams, whose words carry an energy that we know does not belong to our psyche, as when I was told that "He has a special tenderness for His own personal idiots." Sometimes we open a book and know that the words that we read are a message from our Beloved. In so many ways our Beloved speaks to us, answers our prayers, reveals Himself in the inner and outer worlds, "on the horizons and in themselves." There are many ways our Beloved shares with us the wonder of what is real. But words are the most usual way our Beloved communicates to us.

Our listening within the heart attunes us to our Beloved. Divine words have a higher frequency than ordinary discourse; they are more subtle and easily overlooked. By listening within the heart we develop the ear of the heart, the inner listening of the soul that can perceive at this higher frequency. Still, such listening requires both attentiveness and discrimination, as it is not always easy to discriminate between the voice of the ego and the voice of our Beloved. But there is a distinct difference: the words of the ego and mind belong to duality; the words of the heart carry the imprint of oneness. In the heart there is no argument, no you and me, just an unfolding oneness. The heart embraces a difficulty, while the ego takes sides.

Listening, waiting for love's words, turns us away from our own needs to being attentive to His need. In our need we call to our Beloved, and then we wait at the doorway of

11

the heart, listening for an answer. But gradually, imperceptibly, this inner listening becomes more important than our
own need. Our questions become fewer, our inner attention
grows. Once the Beloved begins to nourish us with His
response, the soul's need for companionship is nurtured; the
soul is no longer a starving infant crying in the darkness
of abandonment.

We look to Him and He looks to us. Many times God's
response to our prayers is so deep or so subtle that we do not
notice it—it is not captured by consciousness. But when we
are made aware of divine grace then the inner communion
of the soul with its Maker is brought into consciousness.
Sometimes our Beloved's response is a feeling, an increased
awareness, an intuition. Love may open our heart more fully,
or touch the heart of another. The response may come to
us in the outer world, as a synchronicity that captures our
attention, a change of situation or a healing that is given.

When our Beloved speaks to us, hints to us, then we
know we belong to love, and we begin to feel the security of
this belonging. Love's response carries the intimacy of this
relationship. Even in the times of dryness, when our Beloved
does not speak to us, we carry the memory of His words.
As St. Teresa says, "these words do not vanish from the
memory for a very long time." Then, when in His mercy we
again hear His words, we know that we are known, not just
as part of the great mass of humanity, but as an individual,

with our own unique qualities and needs. Our Beloved has come to us and reminded us that we are loved with special care and tenderness.

We pray to our Beloved who answers us. Knowing that our prayers are heard, we feel the wonder of experiencing that the inner connection of the soul to God exists, not just as an abstract idea, but as a living reality. Being told that God cares for us is very different from experiencing the intimacy and individual nature of this care. The response to our prayers brings into our consciousness, into our daily life, the soul's link to its Beloved. We then no longer believe in God, we *know*.

2
STAGES *of* PRAYER

Mystical prayer draws us into a more and more intimate relationship with our soul and with God. St. Teresa of Avila describes prayer and meditation as the door into the castle of the soul; she compares souls without prayer to people whose bodies are paralyzed.[24] In her autobiography, *The Life of St. Teresa of Jesus*, she outlines four stages of prayer: recollection, quiet, union, and ecstasy. She uses the image of a gardener watering his garden to describe these stages. At the beginning the gardener must make a great effort to draw the water up from the well, but slowly the drawing of the water becomes easier and the effort of the gardener becomes less and less, until in the final stage there is no longer even a gardener, only the Lord Himself soaking the garden in abundant rain.

Once our heart has been turned towards God and awakened to longing, we try to find our way Home. But so often the path is hard and stony. We need to make every effort to stay focused on a goal that appears so distant and inaccessible, when we know the Beloved who called to us, who turned our heart back to love, only as a "sigh in the soul," a sadness and longing for something invisible.

All pilgrims pass along this road, where our only sense of the Beloved is absence, and our pain only amplifies our isolation and loneliness. In this early stage of the journey the cry of the heart seems endless and unanswered, like that of Gerard Manley Hopkins: "And my lament is cries countless, cries like dead letters sent to him that lives alas! away."[25] Only the fire burning in our heart and the knowledge of those who have walked before us keep us putting one foot in front of the other. It is our desperation that drives us forward.

But gradually the pilgrim and the path begin to change. Flowers appear between the hard stones. We slowly sense the closeness of the Beloved. As the veils of separation become thinner, divine presence rather than absence begins to take us Home. Before it was the torment of a world without our Beloved that pushed us along; now it is the fondness of an embrace that draws us Home. The more we come into God's presence the greater the grace, and eventually the path that had required every effort becomes effortless, for "how can there be effort with Divine things? They are given, infused...."[26]

Recollection

The first stage of prayer is the work of keeping our attention on God despite all the distractions of the world. Although our heart is inwardly turned towards God, the world still easily clutches at us with desires and temptations, with our sense of all our unmet needs and lack of fulfillment. Prayer and meditation require effort, constant vigilance. St. Teresa describes this first stage of prayer as watering a garden by drawing the water up from a well with great effort, a task so tiring to the gardener "that he is often unable to move his arms for that purpose, or have one good thought." Beginners in prayer "must be very wearied in keeping the senses recollected, and this is a great labour, because the senses have been hitherto accustomed to distraction."[27]

This is the process of turning away from the world, the negation, in which the inner attention of the seeker is turned away from the outer world and the desires of the ego and back towards the Beloved. It is often a time when we are assailed by doubts and difficulties, as the ego and the mind try to obstruct us and convince us of the uselessness of our quest. Why search for something invisible that demands sacrifice and suffering when this world offers so many visible, tangible attractions? The ego knows that its identity and autonomy are threatened, and so will use all its skills to create every possible confusion and problem to deter us. Furthermore, because the ego is the central part of our consciousness it knows where we are most easily led astray. Nothing knows our weaknesses better than our own self. Nothing can distract us more easily than our own mind.

The ego stands firmly between the seeker and the light that is hidden within. It blocks us from the influence, guidance, and help that come from the soul. It tells us that we are weak and unable to make the journey. Like the birds at the beginning of 'Attār's fable of the quest, *The Conference of the Birds,* it offers innumerable excuses. The nightingale says that he is not strong enough for such a journey, his love for the rose is enough. The duck timidly says that she cannot leave the familiar water to cross the valleys to fly to the Simurgh (the object of the quest), while the partridge is so attached to precious stones that he is not interested in seeking the true jewel. They all say that they do not want to give up their tranquil lives and are too feeble to reach the sublime Simurgh.

In 'Attār's fable the Hoopoe, who is the birds' guide, encourages them to love rather than think about themselves:

He who loves does not think about his own life; to love
truly a man must forget about himself, be he ascetic

or libertine. If your desires do not accord with your spirit, sacrifice them, and you will come to the end of your journey. If the body of desire obstructs the way, reject it; then fix your eyes in front and contemplate.[28]

Love is the desire of the heart that can help us overcome the desires of the ego. St. Paul said, "Love bears all things";[29] love gives us the strength to bear the difficulties, doubts, and uncertainties that the ego and the mind place in our path. If we know ourselves as lovers then we know the meaning of our sacrifice and we can cross the desert that lies between the ego and the Self.

Love helps us to stay true to the essence of our quest in these testing times. Yet so often the heart itself seems barren or closed. St. Teresa says, describing the seeker in this state, "For many days, he is conscious only of aridity, disgust, dislike."[30] This is the time for perseverance, when willpower and determination are needed to see us through. Pride can also be helpful. Not the pride of the ego that says I am better than others, but the dignity of the Self, the instinctual inner nobility of the human being which speaks to the suffering ego and says, "Others have done this before me and I am not less than they." The spiritual path is the most demanding challenge that a human being can face.

Yet in this desert we are being prepared. The focus of our whole psyche is being shifted from the ego to the soul, from the mind to the heart. The dryness that we experience is an effect of our being disengaged from outer fulfillment as this shift takes place. We continue to live our outer life but often it feels without meaning or purpose, nor does the inner world offer any fulfillment. Inwardly we are being realigned with our divine nature and the deepest meaning of the soul. But only when the process is complete can we experience this different level of meaning. In the meantime we suffer the barrenness of being disconnected from the old ego-oriented values and can only trust that this desolation has a higher purpose.

During this time it is as if one door has closed behind us and another has yet to open. Our old world no longer holds our attention; we may even lose our friends as our orientation and our interests change. And yet at the same time the inner world of the soul does not seem to nourish us.

In this first stage, which can last for years, life feels empty because we are being emptied and our attention is being turned towards a world that as yet we cannot see. We are being ground down, until we are thin enough to pass through the narrow door that opens into the spiritual dimension of our own being.

Quiet

Our effort of recollection, our focus on the beyond and our disciplined practice of prayer and meditation make up the thread that guides us across these barren days. Then slowly, imperceptibly, the scene begins to change. As we walk homeward, often going one step backwards for every two we go forward, our Beloved comes to meet us. And for every step we make towards love, love makes ten towards us. At first we do not know this, so great is the apparent distance between us. But one day we realize that the desolation is no longer there. There is a sense of peace that has arrived unnoticed; the wind is not bitter and cold but soft. Irina Tweedie describes how it happened to her:

> And so it came ... it tiptoed itself into my heart, silently, imperceptibly, and I looked at it with wonder. It was still small, a light-blue flame, trembling softly. It had the infinite sweetness of a first love, like an offering of fragrant flowers with gentle hands, the heart full of stillness and wonder and peace.[31]

Our Beloved who we so often thought had betrayed us, whom we had doubted and despaired of, comes to us when we are ready. Without our knowing it the dryness of the desert has opened us. We have shown our Beloved that as lovers we were prepared to endure deprivation, that we would not return to the world just because He seemed to have abandoned us. The Beloved called us to love and then left us in the dark night of our own despair. We cried out, like the poet Hopkins, "No worst, there is none.... Comforter, where is your comforting? Mary, mother of us, where is your relief?"[32] Each of our cries reached our Beloved, our prayers were heard, but love had to wait until we were desperate enough. As a friend was told in a dream, "You must reach the point of total despair." Because only then does the cry of the lover come from the very depths of the soul. Then the grip of the ego is shattered by the need of the heart:

> You'll be free from the trap of your being,
>   when, through spiritual need,
> You're trodden underfoot, like a mat,
>   in the mosque and the wine house.[33]

Yet this experience of desolation and transformation is not a single happening but a process that is repeated many times over as the ego gradually loses its hold. Slowly we die to the world and each death is painful. But as the ego holds our attention less there is more space for the Beloved and for divine love. Each time after a period of darkness, to our amazement, we are given more than we could ever imagine. Each time it becomes easier because we consciously come to know the value of our sacrifice—we know that we suffer in order to come closer to Him. The tenth-century Sufi al-Hallāj, who is known as love's martyr, so deeply understood the relationship between suffering and the Beloved that he could say, "Suffering is He Himself, whereas happiness comes from Him."[34]

In our desolation we suffer the soul's most painful anguish of separation. Then love lifts a veil and gives us a glimpse of our real nature and of the infinite tenderness our Beloved has for us. We begin to feel the sweetness of the spark of divine love that is now present within our heart and soul. We feel nurtured by this light, held by this love. It is a gift from our Beloved, unexpected and infinitely precious. Prayer begins to be a living presence within us, rather than an effort of recollection. More and more we just want to rest deeply in the sweet stillness.

After this our spiritual life changes and we begin to experience divine presence rather than only absence. Once we have glimpsed the light of our divine nature we slowly become blind to the attractions of the world. In the brighter light of our divine nature the ego appears shadowy and insubstantial. We do not reject the world; rather it falls away and we begin to rest in God. St. Teresa describes this as the second degree of prayer, the Prayer of Quiet:

> Herein the soul begins to be recollected; it is now touching the supernatural—for it never could by any efforts of its own attain to this…. As soon as the soul has arrived thus far, it begins to lose the desire of earthly things, and no wonder; for it sees clearly that, even for a moment, this joy is not to be had on earth; that there are no riches, no dominion, no

honours, no delights that can for one instant, even for the twinkling of an eye, minister such a joy; for it is a true satisfaction and the soul sees that it really does satisfy.[35]

At this stage the seeker has begun to surrender to God, who begins to take over. In St. Teresa's image of watering the garden, the gardener, instead of drawing water manually from the well, now has "a machine of wheel and buckets whereby the gardener may draw more water with less labour, and be able to take some rest instead of being continually at work."[36]

Union

Gradually we learn to give our self to our Beloved so that we can be taken into love's mystery. St. Teresa quotes the Bible's poem of mystical love, *The Song of Solomon*: "He brought me to his banqueting house and his banner over me was love." She comments,

We cannot enter by any efforts of our own. His Majesty must put us right into the center of our soul and must enter there Himself; and, in order that He may the better show us His wonders, it is His pleasure that our will, which has entirely surrendered itself to Him, should have no part in this.[37]

This unfolding of prayer, this meeting of love, happens through grace and not through effort. In the hidden place of the heart the soul opens to the Beloved, and the Beloved responds according to His will, as *The Song of Solomon* passionately exclaims:

> I sleep, but my heart waketh: it is the voice of my beloved that knocketh, saying, Open to me, my sister, my love, my dove, my undefiled: for my head is filled with dew, and my locks with the drops of the night....
>
> I rose up to open to my beloved; and my hands dropped with myrrh, and my fingers with sweet smelling myrrh, upon the handles of the lock.
>
> I opened to my beloved; but my beloved had withdrawn himself, and was gone: my soul failed when he spake: I sought him, but I could not find him; I called him but he gave me no answer.[38]

When the Beloved is present the lover experiences a bliss that often has an erotic quality, and the lover is always the receptive one impregnated by the Beloved. When our Beloved is absent our heart waits. In either case the lover's inward attitude is feminine. It is a state of surrender through which the Beloved can enter the lover's heart and life when He wills. At the deepest, most passionate level, this surrender is a state of abandonment in which our soul has given itself completely to its Beloved. In the words of St. Teresa,

> That soul has now delivered itself into His hands
> and His great love has so completely subdued it that
> it neither knows nor desires anything save that God
> shall do with it what He wills. Never, I think, will God
> grant this favour save to the soul which He takes for
> His very own.[39]

The lover becomes the bride of the Beloved, belonging only to Him. The Beloved is invisible but eternally present, and tells the bride the secrets of love that are only shared between lovers. In the depths of the heart love tells us all we need to know, not with words but "whispered in the unspeakable but eloquent silence of God."[40] It is to the bride that the Beloved reveals love's mystery, because it is this inner feminine attitude of surrender that enables the lover to give birth to the Beloved as a living reality within the heart.

As we are drawn deeper and deeper into this inner communion of prayer, we want nothing more than to remain in this state. We are nourished from within, our deepest needs are met, our soul is satisfied. At times we resist having to return from these states, to open our eyes again to the outer world with its many demands and difficulties. We want to remain inwardly absorbed, taken in prayer.

This union of the soul with God belongs to St. Teresa's third stage of prayer. Rather than the mechanism of a wheel and bucket, the gardener uses the water from a stream or river. This third stage of prayer is an extension of the Prayer of Quiet. But rather than just being drawn inward into a state of quiet, our inner and outer life are united:

> In that prayer (the Prayer of Quiet), the soul which would willingly neither stir nor move, is delighting in the holy repose of Mary; but in this prayer it can be like Martha also. Accordingly, the soul is, as it were, leading the active and contemplative life at once, and is able to apply itself to works of charity, and the affairs of its state, and to spiritual reading. Still, those who arrive at this state are not wholly masters of themselves, and are well aware that the better part of the soul is elsewhere. It is as if we were speaking to one person, and another speaking to us at the same time, while we ourselves are not perfectly attentive either to the one or to the other.[41]

This union of the soul embraces all of our life. We are always inwardly waiting, listening, our heart attuned to our Beloved. We are like a piece of wax waiting for an imprint:

> In reality the soul in that state does no more than the wax when a seal is impressed upon it—the wax does not impress itself; it only prepares for the impress: that is, it is soft—and does not even soften itself so as to be prepared; it merely remains quiet and consenting.[42]

But we live this state of receptivity of the soul also in our daily life. Whatever our outer activities, our heart is inwardly attentive. However, this does not make everyday life easier, because our inner attention is always somewhere else. As St. Teresa says, although the soul engages in outer activity, "the better part of the soul is elsewhere. It is as if we were speaking to one person, and another speaking to us at the same time, while we ourselves are not perfectly attentive either to the one or to the other."

The work of the mystic is to live in the two worlds. However much we are engaged in the outer world, we remain inwardly in a state of prayer, resting in God. This practice of constant inner prayer is described in the Qur'an: "Men whom neither business nor profit distract from the recollection of God."[43] And for the Sufi it is expressed in the saying "Outwardly to be with the people, inwardly to be with God."[44] We live amidst the ordinariness as well as the dramas and difficulties of everyday life, with our family and job. And yet we remain inwardly vigilant, our heart awake to the needs of our Beloved.

Ecstasy

In both our inner and outer life, the lover aspires to be attentive to the Beloved, which St. John of the Cross describes as an effortless state:

> [We] must be content with a loving peaceful attentiveness to God, and live without the concern, without the effort, and without the desire to taste or feel Him. All these desires disquiet the soul and distract it from the peaceful quiet and sweet idleness of the contemplation which is being communicated to it.[45]

Yet one can only be fully attentive if one is without desire, even the desire to be with God. Meister Eckhart describes this as true spiritual poverty: "so long as you have any desire to fulfill the will of God and have any hankering after eternity and God, for just so long you are not truly poor."[46] If our attention is to be fully focused on the Beloved we must want nothing for ourselves.

The more we are inwardly attentive to the Beloved the more fully divine love participates in our daily life. The heart's prayer permeates our life and becomes the foundation of our consciousness. In being attentive we allow divine grace to be infused into our lives. It is this grace that changes our life so that we can embrace the Beloved rather than exclude Him. We learn to live with love; we learn its secrets, how it works within the heart and within the world. Our own effort, the effort of "recollection," aligns us with the stream of love that flows between the Creator and the creation. But once we are aligned, this energy effortlessly reveals the secrets within our hearts and within creation.

At first we are not aware of the Beloved's presence and participation in our life, partly because we have become conditioned to think that God is something other than our self. We have also been so conditioned by the very nature of the spiritual quest to be always looking and searching that we tend to turn our attention away from what is present. But the prayer of the heart always returns us to the center of our soul and teaches us the truth of oneness.

As the lover becomes more and more immersed in the Beloved, the greater become the experiences of oneness, of merging with God. Yet the states in this fourth stage of prayer cannot be described or understood by the ordinary mind. Only it can be helpful for the mind to understand that it is unable to understand. Then it will surrender more gladly into these states of unknowingness. As St. Teresa explains, "we understand by not understanding":

> The will must be fully occupied in loving, but it does not understand how it loves; the understand-ing, if it understands, does not understand how it

understands—at least, it can comprehend nothing of that it understands: it does not understand, as it seems to me, because as I said just now, this cannot be understood. I do not understand it at all myself.[47]

The prayer of union becomes a state of deepening absorption in God. St. Teresa, trying to describe this fourth state of prayer, writes that the soul is utterly dissolved in God. Without subject or object, there is "enjoyment without any knowledge of what is being enjoyed."[48] In this sense there is no separate identity and thus there is no one there to make any effort. In her image of watering the garden there is no longer a gardener, only the Lord Himself, and "the rain comes down abundantly to soak and saturate the garden."

Slowly, after all our discipline and inner work, we become familiar with the empty silence that is in the very core of our being. It is here that the prayer of union takes place; a prayer born not from desire or need but from merging in God. Ravished by love, there can be seemingly endless moments of ecstasy that are felt throughout one's whole being, both soul and body. There may be bliss, rapture, or the primal emptiness of unknowing. The lover is then absorbed into the Beloved to such a degree that at times there is not even any consciousness. One just knows that one has been taken by love. One returns from these states often bewildered and confused.

In *The Conference of the Birds* 'Attār describes this stage as the Valley of Astonishment and Bewilderment. He illustrates it with the story of the princess who falls in love with a slave. After drinking a goblet of drugged wine the slave is taken to her chamber, where he spends the night in bliss with her. He is then given another drink of drugged wine and awakes in his own quarters. He is unable to understand what has happened:

> I am in a tumult because what I have seen has happened to me in another body. While hearing nothing I have heard everything, while seeing nothing I have seen everything.... What can be more puzzling than something which is neither revealed nor hidden? What I have seen I can never forget, yet I have no idea where it happened. For one whole night I revelled with a beauty who is without equal. Who or what she is I do not know. Only love remains, and that is all. But God knows the truth.[49]

In the silent niche of the heart the lover experiences the truth that there is only one prayer that underlies all of creation—the prayer in which the Beloved is present, not as a personal God or Creator, but as something both inexpressible and intimate. In this innermost recognition of the heart the lover recognizes the Beloved as something inseparable from himself. And in these moments of absorption only the Beloved exists. This primal awareness of the heart is the foundation of all prayer and all praise. In the words of Rūmī:

> Become silent and go by way of silence toward nonexistence,
> And when you become nonexistent you will be all praise and laud![50]

Through the prayer of the heart the lover inwardly opens to the silence of the soul where the Beloved is always present. Here the lover and Beloved meet, and the lover surrenders into the emptiness. In the formlessness of love we are absorbed deeper and deeper until we are so lost that there is only the ecstasy of unknowing. The anonymous author of *The Cloud of Unknowing* describes this as the "highest part of contemplation" which "hangeth all wholly in this darkness and in this cloud of unknowing; with a loving striving and a blind beholding unto the naked being of God Himself only."[51]

3

THE JESUS PRAYER
and the DHIKR

There is another form of the prayer of the heart within Christianity that is also echoed within the Sufi tradition. This is the "Jesus Prayer" which is practiced in the Orthodox Church,[52] and has profound similarities to the Sufi practice of the *dhikr*, the repetition of a sacred word or phrase, particularly the name of God.

The outward form of the Jesus Prayer is the simple repetition of the phrase "Lord Jesus Christ, Son of God, have mercy on me." There can also be variations. It can be shortened to "Lord Jesus Christ, have mercy on me," or "have mercy on us." And it can be expanded by adding the words "a sinner" at the end. This prayer can be practiced in two ways. In the "free" form of the practice words are repeated throughout the day, whatever one's outer occupation. If one is walking, or engaged in tasks that do not require one's full attention, one can inwardly repeat the prayer, thus ensuring that no moment is wasted from spiritual practice— "the hands at work, the mind and heart with God." The Jesus Prayer can also be practiced in a more "formal" way when one is alone and can focus one's whole inner attention on the prayer, allowing it to take one deeper within, finally into the heart, which is the real home of prayer.

The Sufi *dhikr* is also outwardly a simple repetition. It can be the *shahāda*, "*Lā ilāha illā 'llāh*" (There is no god but God), but it is often one of the names or attributes of God. It is said that God has ninety-nine names, and foremost among these is Allāh: Allāh is His greatest name and contains all His divine attributes. In some Sufi *tarīqas* (paths) the *dhikr* is chanted at group meetings, often with drumming or other music, producing a dynamically powerful and intoxicating effect. In the Naqshbandi Sufi order it is practiced silently and can be repeated throughout the day, as well as at times of focused inner contemplation.[53] The Naqshbandi practice of the silent *dhikr* is the most similar to the Orthodox practice of the Jesus Prayer. Sometimes prayer beads are used to help in the repetition of the *dhikr*, similar to the prayer rope of the Orthodox monk.[54]

The significance the Sufis attribute to the repetition of God's name is illustrated in the story of the eleventh-century Sufi from Nishapur, Abū Sa'īd ibn Abī'l-Khayr, whose heart was opened when he heard the phrase from the Qur'an,

"Say Allāh! then leave them to amuse themselves in their
folly." Abū Sa'īd then retired to the niche of the chapel in
his house, where for seven years he repeated "Allāh! Allāh!
Allāh!"—"until at last every atom of me began to cry aloud,
'Allāh! Allāh! Allāh!'" The day before he first heard the
phrase he had been with Sheikh Abū'l-Fadl Hasan, and
when the Sheikh picked up a book and began to peruse it,
Abū Sa'īd, being a scholar, couldn't help wondering what
the book was. The sheikh perceived his thought and said:

> Abū Sa'īd! All the hundred and twenty-four thousand
> prophets were sent to preach one word. They bade the
> people say "Allāh!" and devote themselves to Him.
> Those who heard this word with the ear alone let it go
> out by the other ear; but those who heard it with their
> souls imprinted it on their souls and repeated it until
> it penetrated their hearts and souls, and their whole
> being became this word. They were made independent
> of the pronunciation of the word, they were released
> from the sound and the letters. Having understood
> the spiritual meaning of this word, they became so
> absorbed in it that they were no more conscious of
> their own non-existence.[55]

Through the practice of the *dhikr* the Sufi aspires to remember God in every moment, with each and every breath.

This remembrance does not belong to the mind. It is not an act of mental recall, but is the remembrance of the heart, an awareness of our innermost state of union with God. The practice of the *dhikr* may begin with the mental repetition of the name of God, but the divine name takes us deep within the heart, where it helps to bring the hidden secret of divine union into consciousness:

> There are different levels of remembrance and each has different ways. Some are expressed outwardly with audible voice, some felt inwardly, silently, from the center of the heart. At the beginning one should declare in words what one remembers. Then stage by stage the remembrance spreads throughout one's being—descending to the heart then rising to the soul; then still further it reaches the realm of the secrets; further to the hidden; to the most hidden of the hidden. How far the remembrance penetrates, the level it reaches, depends solely on the extent to which Allāh in His bounty has guided one.[56]

Similarly in the Orthodox Church there are three levels of prayer: "prayer of the lips (oral prayer); prayer of the *nous*, the mind or intellect (mental prayer); prayer of the heart."[57] The Jesus Prayer may begin:

... like any other prayer, as an oral prayer, in which the words are spoken by the tongue through a deliberate effort of will ... In the course of time and with the help of God our prayer becomes more inward ... [until] the Name is invoked silently, without any movement of the lips, by the mind alone. When this occurs we have passed, by God's grace, from the first level to the second.... But the journey inwards is not yet complete.... To accomplish the journey inwards and to attain true prayer, it is required of us to enter into this "absolute center," that is, to descend from the intellect into the heart.[58]

It is only within the heart that the Invocation of the Name becomes fully alive, that the prayer of the pilgrim becomes the prayer of Another, the prayer of Jesus that is now awake within the heart. The author of *The Way of A Pilgrim*, who describes his journey of practicing the Jesus Prayer, writes how: "Early one morning the Prayer woke me up as it were."[59] From the effort of the initial practice comes the "self-acting" prayer. The name repeats itself; the mystery of "pray without ceasing" begins to take place within the heart.[60] But it is stressed that this awakening of the prayer of the heart comes not through effort or will, but through the grace of God.

Through repeating His name we remember Him, not just in the mind but also in the heart, and finally for the Sufi there comes the time when every cell of the body repeats the *dhikr*, repeats His name. It is said, "First you do the *dhikr* and then the *dhikr* does you." In the midst of life's outer activities you may stop and, looking within, find the name of God being said within you, or wake up in the night and experience your heart saying the name of the One you love. The *dhikr* gradually becomes a part of our whole being, our conscious and unconscious self, until it sings in our bloodstream. This is beautifully (and literally!) illustrated in an old Sufi story:

> Sahl said to one of his disciples: Strive to say continuously for one day: "O Allāh! O Allāh! O Allāh!" and do the same the next day and the day after that—until he became habituated to saying these words. Then he bade him to repeat them at night also, until they became so familiar that he uttered them even during his sleep. Then [Sahl] said, "Do not repeat them any more, but let all your faculties be engrossed in remembering God!" The disciple did this until he became absorbed in the thought of God. One day, ... a piece of wood fell on his head and broke it. The drops of blood which trickled to the ground bore the legend, "Allāh! Allāh! Allāh!"[61]

Orthodox tradition describes in a similar manner how the repetition of the name permeates the whole being of the practitioner: "Like a drop of ink that falls on blotting paper, the act of prayer should spread steadily outwards from the conscious and reasoning center of the brain until it embraces every part of ourselves."[62]

Inner Transformation

In either tradition the way that the name of God permeates the pilgrim is not metaphoric, but a literal happening. From the initial process of mental repetition the name goes deep within, into our psyche. Working in the depths of our being it alters our mental, psychological, and even physical bodies—everything becomes infused with the energy of the name. On the mental level this change is easily apparent. Normally, in our everyday life, the mind follows its automatic thinking process, over which we often have very little control. The mind thinks us, rather than the other way around. Just catch your mind for a moment and observe its thoughts. Every thought creates a new thought, every answer a new question. And because energy follows thought, our mental and psychological energy is scattered in many directions. Spiritual life means learning to become one-pointed, to focus all our energy in one direction, towards the One. Through repeating the name we alter the grooves of our mental conditioning, the grooves which like those on a record play the same tune over and over again, repeating the same patterns that bind us in our mental habits. The

Jesus Prayer or *dhikr* gradually replaces these many old grooves with the single groove of the divine name. To quote Theophan the Recluse, "To stop the constant jostling of your thoughts, you must bind the mind with one thought, or the thought of One only."[63]

How the prayer or *dhikr* works psychologically is more mysterious. There is a saying of the Prophet Muhammad: "There is a polish for everything that takes away rust; and the polish for the heart is the invocation of Allāh." The name of God is a powerful agent of inner transformation. It is like a catalyst of the inner alchemical process that turns our lead into gold. Its constant repetition goes deep into the unconscious where it both purifies and transforms. This process works partly to align our psyche with our divine nature, which is the real agent of any transformation. Psychologically, it is the Self that transforms us. This center of divine consciousness within us works in the unconscious, disentangling and freeing us from complexes and patterns of conditioning. One example is the marked effect the prayer or *dhikr* can have on fear or anxiety, feelings that often beset the spiritual traveler. Repeating His name can help to dissolve these feelings and the hold they have on us.

The name of God can also be used in a more conscious, directed manner. In my own practice I have found that I can focus the *dhikr* on a problem or psychological block, allowing the feelings, the pain, anger or difficulty, to be contained by the energy of the divine name. This can help bring these feelings to the surface without their being overwhelming. Gradually the energy of the *dhikr* transforms this inner darkness, freeing me from a constriction, giving me access to more energy, allowing more inner space for the Divine. I found that doing this practice while walking was most helpful and grounding, when the rhythm of my footsteps and the rhythm of the *dhikr* allowed me to turn inward and focus on the slow and gradual work of polishing the heart.

Some of the potency of the Jesus Prayer and the *dhikr* lies in the power of the name. In a traditional or sacred language the name contains the essence of that which is named. To know a person's name allows you access to her true nature, to her soul. That is why in traditional cultures there is often a taboo against telling your name to someone who is not a close family member. The magical relationship between the name and a person is evident in the story of Rumpelstiltskin, who loses his power when his name is known. The same tradition is evident in the response of the angel to Manoah, "Why askest thou after my name, seeing it is secret?"[64]

Invoking the name of God can give one access to the power of the Divine. In Christianity people are healed through the name of Jesus, and the potency of this name is expressed in Christ's promise at the Last Supper: "Whatever you shall ask the Father in my Name, He will give it to you."[65] The power of the divine name (in this case the name of the

Father) is also evident in the Lord's Prayer, "Hallowed be Thy Name." The constant repetition of the divine name, whether Jesus or God the Father or Allāh or any of the other names by which we invoke the Divinity, aligns us with the source of divine energy and power that is within us. Without this energy there can be no real inner transformation.

We always need to remember that this work on the soul is something we do together with God. Repeating the name of the One we love reminds us of this primal companionship, this intimate friendship. One might imagine it would be boring to repeat one name over and over again for the rest of one's life. But how can you become bored with the name of the One you love, the name of the One to whom you belong? Every repetition is an offering of love, a recognition of this link of love that is within everything.

The Breath

Both the Jesus Prayer and the *dhikr* are often practiced in conjunction with the breath. In the Jesus Prayer often the first part, "Lord Jesus Christ, Son of God," is said while drawing in the breath, and the second part, "have mercy on me," while breathing out.[66] However, some Orthodox teachers advise against too much focus on breathing techniques, suggesting rather that one should just have "quiet and steady breathing."[67] The breath is more central to the *dhikr*—and different Sufi orders teach different breathing practices in conjunction with the repetition of sacred words. In the Naqshbandi order the repetition of Allāh begins on the out-breath "Al," while "lāh" is repeated on the in-breath.[68]

Breathing is the most primal rhythm of our life, along with the beating of the heart. With every breath we bring vital oxygen into our blood and body. The breath is also central to many spiritual practices. The Naqshbandi Sufis teach that awareness of breath is the foundation of inner work: "The more that one is able to be conscious of one's breathing, the stronger is one's inner life."[69] Through the practice of the *dhikr* we are aware of each and every breath, which is imprinted with our remembrance of God. Through this simple but foundational practice we bring our awareness and remembrance of the Divine into the bloodstream, into our body, psyche, and whole life.

The soul has also been long thought to be in the breath, and is sometimes visualized as a breath-body. In Naqshbandi Sufi teachings the soul comes into the body with every out-breath, and with each in-breath returns to its spiritual dimension. This is expressed in the cycle of the *dhikr*, the conscious return to God in each and every breath. For example, in the Naqshbandi path which focuses on the uncreated emptiness or nothingness of God,[70] there is an esoteric translation of the word Allāh as "the nothing," with the first syllable, "Al" as the article "the," and the second syllable "lāh" as "nothing." So with the in-breath one makes a conscious return to the nothingness, from the world of forms to the formless.[71] The practitioner can also experience a moment of bliss at the end of every in-breath as the soul returns to its natural state, our essential oneness with the Divine.[72]

The breath is the bridge between the outer physical world and the inner world of the soul. While we are alive, with each cycle of the breath the soul makes its journey into this world and then back to God. The mystic aspires to make this journey conscious. This journey is the lived prayer of the soul, an offering of our self to the mystery of life and its all-embracing relationship to God. Repeating the name of the One we love, we consciously connect the two worlds, the inner world of the spirit and the physical world. With each breath we are present in the love affair that is the relationship between the Creator and the creation.

Our work, our practice, and our prayer is to live the link of love between the Creator and the creation. With every breath the name goes into our heart, our body and our blood, where it purifies and empties us, giving more space for the presence of the Divine.[73] The power of the name and its connection to the love that belongs to God is a mystical secret, because it expresses the union between the Creator and the creation. Through the name we bring into consciousness the bond we always had with our

Beloved and become aware of the deeper secrets of our real unity. Our prayer brings the imprint of the heart into the world of time and also leads us back to God. Gradually we become conscious of the depth of our connection, of our union with God that has always existed within our heart.

Creation's Prayer

The repetition within the heart takes us from the forms and images of the outer world to the formless silence that is within us. Even when words are repeated, we experience a stillness within the heart, and we learn to rest in this stillness. And yet while the remembrance of the heart absorbs us into this inner state, it also embraces the outer world. This experience is described in *The Way of A Pilgrim*:

> And when … I prayed with my heart, everything around me seemed delightful and marvelous. The trees, the grass, the birds, the earth, the air, the light seemed to be telling me they existed for man's sake, that they witnessed to the love of God for man, that everything proved the love of God for man, that all things prayed to God and sang His praise.[74]

For the Sufi, invoking His name reveals the secret of oneness within the heart and within life as expressed in the Qur'anic saying (2:115), "Wheresoever you turn, there is the Face of God." Everything is an expression, a manifestation, of the One Being—there is nothing other than God. When the eye of the heart opens we experience everything illumined with divine presence. This light lifts the veil in creation, allowing us to see and participate in the real nature of life—a love affair in which the Beloved reveals Himself through life's myriad forms. The mystic can then glimpse the prayer that is present in all of creation, as Dhū'l-Nūn witnessed:

> Whoever recollects God in reality, forgets all else beside Him, because all the creatures recollect Him, as is witnessed by those who experience a revelation. I experienced this state from evening prayer until one third of the night was over, and I heard the voices of the creatures in the praise of God, with elevated voices so that I feared for my mind. I heard the fishes who said: Praised be the King, the Most Holy, the Lord.[75]

The Jesus Prayer and the Sufi *dhikr* may begin with the effort of repeating a phrase or a word, but these words penetrate deep within the heart where they become an intimate communion, in which the power of the name invokes the One whom we love. Through love's presence we may come to experience how the prayer in our heart is a part of the prayer of the whole of creation, just as His name is inscribed in every cell of existence. The wonder of this world is that it belongs to God, that it looks towards the One in praise and longing, constantly affirming the existence of the Divine. All of life is a song of remembrance of which our heart, soul, and body make up just a small note of love.

4

THE CIRCLE *of* LOVE

The First Prayer

The mystical path takes the wayfarer on the journey of the soul that begins with the experience of being separate from God and the awakening of the soul's primal longing to return Home, and leads ultimately to the realization of oneness: that lover and Beloved are one, and always were one. Separation is an illusion created by the ego and its identity as a separate self. The journey Home is a return journey in which we "die" to this false-self and rediscover our essential union with God. We travel this circle of love with our prayers and devotions, with the deep longing of the heart to come to know the primal mystery of oneness that belongs to all of creation.

Prayer is a central part of this journey in which we turn away from the ego and its many desires and go deep within the heart. Here the lover enters the sacred space that belongs to the most intimate relationship of the soul with God. This is the place of real prayer, where we are alone with our Beloved. Our prayers may begin with words, with speaking within our heart to our Beloved of our longings, our difficulties, our needs. But as the journey continues, as we are drawn further and further into the circle of love, our words fade away as we begin to taste the truth of oneness. And finally we realize the mystery of prayer, that it was always the Beloved calling out within our heart: there was only One crying out to Itself. In the words of Rūmī:

> It is he who suffers his absence in me
> Who through me cries out to himself.
> Love's most strange, most holy mystery—
> We are intimate beyond belief.[76]

The real nature of mystical prayer is to draw us into this most intimate mystery of divine love. The mystic comes to know that the essence of prayer is this hidden secret of the heart—that there is only oneness. For when the heart is open and looks towards God it is awakened to the revelation of divine unity—"I am He whom I love, He whom I love is me." This state of prayer is a merging and melting that transcends the mind and its notions of duality: the heart overwhelms us with divine presence that obliterates any sense of our own self.

These moments of prayer are moments of union, in which the lover is lost. We have stepped from the shore of our own being into the limitless ocean of the Beloved. We make this offering out of devotion and selflessness, out of the heart's need to share its secret. Standing on the shore, we cry out our need to be with our Beloved, our need to talk, to share our troubles and joys. But when the Beloved comes close, we enter the ocean of divine presence where our words, along with our mind, fade away, dissolved into oneness.

When love reveals its real nature we come to know that there is neither lover nor Beloved. There is no one to pray and no one to pray to. We do not even know that we are lost; we return from these states of merging knowing only that we gave our self and were taken. Our gift of our self was accepted so completely that we knew nothing of the encounter. We looked towards our Beloved and were taken into love's arms, embraced in oneness, dissolved in nearness. For so many years we had cried and called out, and when the Beloved finally came the meeting was so intimate there was nothing left of us to witness it.

But when we return from this merging of oneness, when the mind again surrounds us, we can see the footprints that led us to this shore, to the place where the two worlds meet. We can tell stories of the journey that led us to the edge of the heart's infinite ocean, of the nights we called out, and the tears we cried in our calling, of our need that was for so many years all that we knew, a need born of the despair of separation, the deepest despair known to the soul.

This need was our first prayer, planted in the soul by the One who loves us, who wants us. This need of the soul is the bond of love, the mystic's pledge to remember God. We awaken to this remembrance with the knowledge of our forgetfulness, the experience of separation. We are made to experience that we are separate from our Beloved, that we have forgotten Him. This experience brings into consciousness our soul's need to return Home, to journey from separation to union. The first prayer is the sigh in the soul, the reed flute's lament that it has been torn from the reed-bed and longs to return.[77]

This first prayer is deep within us. Often we feel it only indistinctly, as the mind and ego block us from the potency of its message. Buried in the heart, in its innermost chamber, lover cries to Beloved, and we feel the muffled echo of this cry as an unhappiness, a discontent. Subtly it torments us, and we often try to avoid it, to run away from its primal sorrow. The world is full of so many distractions, the mind and psyche full of so many patterns of avoidance. But gradually, or in some cases suddenly, we know that we have to go Home, that we have to honor our longing; we need to bring the prayer of the heart into our consciousness.

What began in the heart is passed to the tongue: "Oh Beloved, help me. I am so alone and I need you." The prayer is then made conscious: we live this prayer with the words we cry. With all the power and limitations of language, we speak our need, and so come to know our despair. With the simple words of our prayers we make conscious the pain of separation, and so call out even more, knowing in the depths that we will be heard: "I respond to the call of the caller when he calls to Me." (Qur'an 2:186)

This prayer, born of longing, is so simple, giving voice to the heart's pain. Each in our own way we make this prayer; we bring into our life the soul's sigh. And each time we pray, each time our heart calls out, we engrave this longing more firmly into consciousness. The potency of words is that they belong to this world, to the world of our mind and ego. In the dimension of union there is no word; communication is communion, an unfolding of oneness. In the world of separation we need words, even to speak to our Beloved. When we speak our prayers we acknowledge that we are separate and needy. We state the gulf, the abyss between us. With each word we come to know our longing more consciously.

Sometimes Sufis call with spontaneous prayer, *du'ā*, the free prayer of the heart, which is the intimate conversation of lovers. Or they may call with ritual prayer, *salāt*, which for the mystic is a time of connection, "the moment of proximity to God."[78] Or the dervish may repeat the inward prayer of remembrance, the sacred syllables of the *dhikr*, the repetition of the name of the One we love. In these ways we make known our need, make it known to our self as well as to our Beloved. And in this moment of prayer we enter into divine presence. In the words of Kharrāz, "When entering on prayer you should come into the Presence of God … stand before Him with no mediator between."[79]

Yet prayer, born of need, does not answer this need—it makes it more potent. We come to know more fully that we are separate, and that only our Beloved can help us. We pray to our idea of the Divine: some concept of a distant God, or a kind father-figure, or a nurturing mother, someone who will wash away our tears and look after us, or even sometimes to an antagonistic tyrant. We personify our longing, clothe our tears in our image of a deity or a lost love. In our weakness we look for strength, in our sorrow a comforting shoulder, in our pain a tormentor.

We make an image of the Divine to suit us, to give us comfort and security, to contain the pain of being human. But as our prayer deepens all images gradually fall away, for they too are veils of separation, denying the truth of union. How can the Beloved be separate? Who calls out to whom? There is only One. Then we come to glimpse the reality behind the images, that our need is God's need, that our cry is itself the Beloved's answer: "Thy calling 'Allāh!' was My 'Here I am,' thy yearning pain My messenger to thee."[80]

The mystery of the path is that in the closed circle of love the Beloved calls to Himself within the heart of the lover. Our need is His need, and yet He is complete in every way. We carry the seed of divine longing and make it our own. Our very prayer to come closer to our Beloved is an unfolding of intimacy, a sharing of something infinitely precious. The Beloved needs our tears, our cries, our longing, our prayers. He shares this secret with us. He calls to us and we call to Him, and so love reveals itself. Through our prayers what was hidden within the heart becomes part of everyday life, part of the texture of the world. We are burdened with the pain and bliss of living this secret.

Standing at the Doorway

The heart is the chamber of love's oneness, the infinite inner space where the Beloved is always present. Prayer leads us to the door of the heart, where we learn to wait with patience. We long for our prayers to be answered, for our need to be met. But always in prayer there is a quality of surrender: "Only if it is according to Thy will." Even in our most desperate moments prayer is a bowing down before God.

Surrendering to divine will, we acknowledge God's presence behind the door. We allow love to work according to its own ways. Sometimes we will be answered, and sometimes not. Sometimes we will be made to wait, sometimes left with all the desperation of our prayer. Why does the Beloved seem to ignore those whom He loves? Because He wants them to call upon Him. He loves to hear their voice. "It is related that Yahya b. Sa'id al-Qattan saw God in his

57

sleep and exclaimed, 'O my God, how many times I have prayed to You and You have not answered me!' He said, 'O Yahya, this is because I love hearing your voice.'"[81]

If our need were answered fully and completely, we would no longer look to our Beloved, no longer call out. God knows how to draw us back to Him, "with the drawing of this Love and the voice of this Calling."[82] Through our prayers our Beloved calls us homeward, whether our prayers appear to be answered or not. On this journey our prayers carry the fragrance of divine love back to us.

Praying within the heart, we stand at the doorway between the two worlds, waiting for our Beloved to help us. The One who is our innermost essence is always there, eternally watching, listening, waiting for us to come. We think God is separate from us, because we stand outside the door, caught in the world of duality. But when we pray with feeling, pray with the intensity of the heart, then the door opens. Actually this door is never closed; the ego only drew its veil across the threshold:

> Salih al-Murri [said], "Whoever is persistent in knock-
> ing at the door is on the verge of having it opened
> for him."
>
> Rābi'a asked him, "How long are you going to say
> this? When was the door closed so that one had to
> ask to have it opened?"[83]

The intensity of our feeling takes us beyond the ego. The stronger our need and the greater our longing, the more the heart cries out. This is why Ibn 'Arabī prayed, "Oh Lord nourish me not with love but with the desire for love."[84] He knew that this desire would tear away the veils of separation and reveal what is hidden. The veils themselves create the separation, distracting us from the reality of our oneness with God, catching our attention in a world of multiplicity. Need turns us inward, away from these myriad reflections towards the Source, the oneness that is the root of our desire.

Love hears our call and opens the door that is never closed. We are heard by our own heart, and our need is answered by love. Love is drawn by need, as Rūmī so poignantly writes:

> Not only the thirsty seek the water,
> the water as well seeks the thirsty.[85]

Love, the greatest power in the universe, does more than heal hearts. Love is the vehicle for divine grace, the means of divine mercy. Love brings both understanding and nearness, both wisdom and comfort.

Prayer is an ablution of the heart, for it takes us into the purifying stream of love that flows at the core of creation, the stream of "He loves them and they love Him" (Qur'an 5:54). In our prayer we are purified by our remembrance of God rather than by any desire for purity. The following dream beautifully images this purifying quality of prayer:

> I am in the courtyard of a very ancient mosque. From
> an old black tap crystal clear water is running down
> on my hands, which are as if in prayer. I am having
> an ablution. The whole of me feels very ancient....
> It is as if I am inwardly merging into this beautiful
> water while every atom in me is singing His prayer.
> I become purer and purer.

In the sacred space of her own heart the dreamer prays, and her prayer is an ablution, an ablution in which the sacred water of her devotion runs down onto her hands, purifying her. Hers is the deepest prayer of merging, a prayer without words in which she gives herself into her prayer so completely that she hears every atom of her being singing His prayer. The potency in her prayer is the purifying power of love and devotion, a devotion that belongs to every atom of herself. This is a prayer born of oneness that carries the power of His love.

The Closed Circle of Love

There comes the time on the mystical journey when prayer embraces all of our life. We are always inwardly in a state of prayer. We speak to our Beloved of our needs and difficulties and give thanks for the help we are given either directly in the heart or, often unexpectedly, outwardly in our daily life. We speak with the intimacy of real friendship, cry with the tears of a lover. We repeat the name of the One we love, to whom we belong, until this name repeats itself within our heart. And deeper than any words there is a meeting and merging within the silence of the heart. Our heart is always turned to our Beloved; we are always listening, waiting, communing. How can one not live a life of prayer when we have so much need, when so much is given?

As the heart's prayer deepens we merge more and more within the heart, into the oneness that is our divine promise. We step from the shores of our own aloneness, our sense of separation, into love's ocean where we are always with our Beloved, sometimes so merged in this ocean, so drowned in love, that there is no sense of self. And yet always we seem to return, to our need, our inadequacies, our limitations. This seems to be part of our human nature and the very nature of prayer: we need and we cry out. Even when we realize the secret of oneness we still need: we are still human. And our prayers are always heard. Even when it appears that they are unanswered they are still heard.

Part of the mystery of divine oneness is that our prayer, our crying out, is needed. There is only one prayer, the prayer of the creation to the Creator. Each in our

61

own way we live this prayer so that the Divine can come to know Its own need. The more intense, the more full of feeling the call, the more clearly this need is heard. Through our prayers the Beloved hears the heart's need, the need of the lover for the Beloved, the need of the creation for the Creator—the Beloved's own need. Our human mystery is to embrace and live this paradox: that we appear to be separate from God and thus in need of the Divine even though we are never separate. But we all know and live this need, and through our prayers give it as an offering back to our Beloved.

We may hope for, long for, desperately need an answer to our prayers. But the deeper truth is that there is only One, crying out in prayer, hearing Its own prayer. The prayer of the heart offers this truth, the secret of secrets, back to the Beloved. This is the closed circle of love that we live through our longing, through our need, through our prayers.

5

THE HEART PRAYS

Prayer turns us away from the outer world to the inner mystery of the soul. Prayer takes us into this sacred inner space. Here the mystic begins to witness one of the greatest wonders that can happen to a human being, the birth of the Beloved within the heart. In esoteric Christian symbolism this is the birth of Christ that takes place within our own heart, as Angelus Silesius expresses very simply:

> If in your heart you make
>   a manger for his birth,
> then God will once again
>   become a child on earth.[86]

We begin the path with the image of the wayfarer, the pilgrim, making a journey back to God. But as we give our self to the longing within the heart, something completely different and unexpected takes place. Our longing, the primal sorrow of the soul, together with our spiritual practices, create a space where the Beloved can be born as a living presence. Our longing is a process of purification that allows for a virgin birth to take place within us. As Rūmī says: "Sorrow for His sake is a treasure in my heart. My heart is Light upon light, a beautiful Mary with Jesus in the womb."[87] "Light upon light" points to the esoteric mystery of how the light of our longing, our desire for our Beloved, meets the greater light of our divine nature. From this meeting of light a child is conceived and then born.

This is a mystical birth in which the Divine, or Christ principle, is born and then lives within the heart of the mystic, the one who has given herself to love. The receptive soul, initially experienced as a place of inner listening, becomes the place into which the Beloved is born as a living presence. The symbol of the virgin birth images the spiritual purity that is needed to allow this to happen. Love and longing have emptied us of all except the desire for God. This is the poverty of the heart that wants nothing for itself:

> I offer to Thee the only thing I have,
> My capacity to be filled with Thee.[88]

Spiritual awakening never happens to the wayfarer. The seeker always remains behind on the shores of love.

Although we may at times have the illusion of developing a spiritual self, real spiritual awakening is the awakening of the heart in which the Divine comes alive within us. Our outer self, even our outer life, may appear to remain as before. But in the depths of our being something fundamental has changed. We have become an empty space where this miracle of love can happen. In the words of the lover Majnun in the great Sufi tale of Layla and Majnun, "Love has moved in and adorned the house. My self tied up its bundle and left."[89] On the Sufi path this is when the "journey to God," becomes the "journey in God."[90]

This birth of the Beloved never happens through our own will or desire, but only through the grace of God. We have to make every effort to purify our self and to surrender. But this inner miracle is always a gift that is given, a gift of which we are always undeserving. Initially our ego-self may not be fully aware of what has happened, of how the very nature of our prayer and devotion has changed. But we feel that something is different, that our heart is alive in a new way.

The heart of the mystic has become a place of divine presence. Our heart becomes a place of prayer that is fully alive, and our life a vehicle for love and the work of this love in the world. As our innermost self has been taken over by love, our heart no longer belongs to us. Although the greatest joy, this is also the greatest sacrifice, a sacrifice beyond that of the ego. For how valuable is that insignificant self with its desires, problems, and dramas? The sacrifice of the heart is an offering of what is most valuable within us. We have given our heart to our Beloved for love to use as It wills. We have truly become a slave of love.

In many ways this is really the beginning of mystical life, when the life of the spirit is fully awakened within us. Little then can be said of this continuing journey in love, because words belong to the outer world and to the mind, and this is a very different reality, one that belongs mainly to silence. But the essence of our prayer changes, because now it is the heart that prays within us, without ceasing.[91] Our ego-self remains behind to live in the outer world. And it will of course at times encounter difficulties, and we will still ask for help and for understanding, still pray for others and pray for the world. But a deeper dimension of prayer has taken over the core of our being, a prayer that is always alive. Once the heart has been awakened to divine presence it remains awake; it remains a place of constant prayer. This is the hidden nature of the heart that belongs to God. It is a place of God's prayer in the world.[92]

The journey continues, the states of love change, the emptiness deepens and the demands of service increase. We learn what it means to live a life that belongs to love. St. Teresa describes this as real spiritual life, belonging to the innermost mansion of the soul:

Do you know when people really become spiritual? It
is when they become slaves of God and are branded
with His sign, which is the sign of the Cross in [which]
they have given Him their freedom.[93]

Sufis describe this state as being "branded by love": the
name of God is written in fire on the heart, and our heart
then forever belongs to our Beloved. Sufis are also known
as "the slaves of God."

The heart prays, no longer the prayer of our need and
longing, but the prayer of our Beloved. This prayer that
takes place in the heart of God's lover belongs to the prayer
of the world itself, and to the deepest relationship between
the creation and the Creator—the divine love affair that is
life itself.[94] Our ego-self may never know the real nature of
this prayer, as it belongs to the secret nature of love, which
is often veiled from consciousness. But we may sense that
a mystery is taking place within us. We may awaken in the
night, or turn inward for a moment during a busy day, and
notice that our heart is at prayer. We have given our heart
in service to our Beloved to be used as love wills. This is
our sacrifice and deepest service. Our heart has become a
place of continual prayer.

6
PRAYER *for the* EARTH

Prayer is a response to a need, our need, the Beloved's need, and at this present time most pressingly, the need of the earth. In whatever way we are drawn to pray, there is a vital need to include the earth in our prayers. We are living in a time of ecological devastation, the catastrophic effect of our materialistic culture on the ecosystem. Our rivers are toxic, the rainforests slashed and burned, vast tracts of land made a wasteland due to our insatiable desires for oil, gas, and minerals. We have raped and pillaged and polluted the earth, pushing it into the dangerous state of imbalance we call climate change. Creation itself is now calling to us, sending us signs of its imbalance, and the soul of the world, the *anima mundi,* which the ancients understood as the spiritual presence of the earth, is crying out. We can see these signs in all the recent floods and droughts, feel it in the poisoning of the land from pesticides and other contaminants. Those whose hearts are open may hear it too, in the cry of the world soul, of the spiritual being of our mother the earth. It is a cry of need and despair: human beings, who were supposed to be the guardians of the planet, who long ago were taught the sacred names of creation,[95] have forgotten their responsibility and instead have systematically and heedlessly desecrated and destroyed the earth on a global scale. And now the earth and its waters are dying.

We are the children and inheritors of a culture that has banished God to heaven. Early Christianity persecuted and ultimately largely extinguished any earth-based spirituality, and the physical world became a place of darkness and sin. Then after the Age of Enlightenment, the prevailing world view that grew out of Newtonian physics framed the world as an inanimate mechanism we could easily master, indeed were meant to master; we simply needed to discover its laws to tame it to our own ends. As a legacy of that view we have developed a materialistic culture that treats the earth as a commodity that exists to serve our own selfish purpose. Our greed now walks with heavy boots across the world, with complete disregard for the sacred nature of creation. We have cared only for our own material comforts and well-being, and as a result live in a dying world whose soul cries to us in despair. And yet, because for centuries we have been taught to see ourselves as separate from the world and the world as just an object we should try to control, we have forgotten that it even has a soul. We have cut ourselves off from the living world in all its interconnectedness. Our Western culture no longer knows how to relate to the world as a sacred being.

Now the world needs our prayers more than we know. It needs us to acknowledge its sacred nature, to understand that it is not just something to use and dispose of. It needs us to help it to reconnect with its own sacred source, the life-giving waters of creation that can save it from destruction. It needs us to remember it to the Creator. We are needed now to reclaim our sacred duty as guardian, or vice-regent,[96] of the natural world. Externally we must help the earth return to balance, help our ecosystem to physically heal itself. And within our own hearts and souls we must help to redeem what has been desecrated: we are needed to pray for the earth and all its creatures.

In our prayers and devotions we need to reconnect with the sacred substance in creation, what the Sufis refer to as the "secret of the word '*Kun!*' ('Be!')." We need to place the earth within our hearts and nourish it with our love and offer it in remembrance to God. We know how to pray for our own troubles; we have cried the tears of our own pain of separation and turned in our despair back to our Beloved. Now we must do the same for the earth with which we are so interconnected, which sustains and nourishes us even as we abuse it. We need to reaffirm the bond of love between the

Creator and the creation, just as we need to affirm our own bond with our Beloved. The mystic knows that only divine love can heal and transform what has been so neglected and abused. Love is the greatest power in creation and through our prayers we can help to bring this love into life, into the planet, into its soil and rivers. Through our prayers we can once again honor the Divine as a living force within creation.

If we acknowledge our sacred role as guardians of the planet we will see the power of our prayers, our capacity to reconnect the earth to its sacred nature just as we have cut it off. Through our hearts and souls we can reunite spirit and matter; our prayers can bring grace and love where they are most needed within the world. Many of us know the effectiveness of prayers for others, have seen how healing and help are given, even in the most unexpected ways. The world is part of our being and needs our prayers too. The world needs the grace that can only come from its Creator. It is in such a desperate state that it needs the miracles that can only come from God. And human beings are the connection between the worlds. Our prayers can be the prayers of the whole of creation, reconnecting heaven and earth.

There are many ways to pray for the earth. First it is essential to acknowledge that the earth is not "unfeeling matter" but a living being that has given us life. It can be helpful to ask ourselves, how would we like to be treated just as a physical object to be used and repeatedly abused?

Then perhaps we can sense the earth's suffering: the physical suffering we see in the dying species and polluted waters, the deeper suffering of our collective disregard for its sacred nature. Perhaps, if we open our hearts and souls to the being we call the world, we will be able to hear the cry of the *anima mundi*, of its soul. For centuries it was understood that the world was a living being with a soul, and that we were a part of this being, the light of our own soul a spark, a *scintilla*, of the light of the world soul.[97] As a culture we have forgotten that, but this understanding is the foundation of the prayer that is needed now. Through it we make that connection conscious once again; we help bring our light back to the world soul.

Once we remember in our minds and in our hearts that the world is a sacred being of which we are a part, once we hear its cry, our prayers will flow more easily and naturally. We will be drawn to pray, each in our own way. One simple way is to place the world as a living being within our hearts when we inwardly offer our self to God. We remember the sorrow and suffering of the world to the Creator, and ask that the world be remembered, that divine love and mercy flow where they are needed. We pray that "His mercy be greater than His justice," that even though we continue to treat the world so badly, God will help us and help the world—help to bring the earth back into balance. We need to remember that the power of the Divine is more than that of all the global corporations that continue to make the world a wasteland, even more than the global forces of consumerism that demand the life-blood of the planet. We pray that our Beloved can redeem and heal this beautiful and suffering world.

Sometimes it is easier to pray when we feel the earth in our hands, when we work in the garden tending our flowers or vegetables. Or when we cook, cutting up the vegetables that the earth has given us, mixing in the herbs and spices that give us pleasure. Or making love, as we share our body and bliss with our lover, we may feel the tenderness and power of creation, how a single spark can give birth. Then our lovemaking can be an offering to life itself, a fully felt remembrance of the ecstasy of creation.

The divine oneness of life is within and all around us. Sometimes walking alone in nature we can feel its heartbeat and its wonder, and our steps become steps of remembrance. The simple practice of "walking in a sacred manner" in which with every step we take we feel the connection with the sacred earth is another way to reconnect with the living spirit of the earth.

There are so many ways to pray for creation, to listen within and include the earth in our practice. Watching the simple wonder of a dawn can be a prayer in itself. Or when we hear the chorus of birds in the morning we may sense that deeper joy of life and awaken to its divine nature. At night the stars can remind us of what is infinite and eternal within us and within the world. Whatever way we are drawn to wonder or pray, what matters is always the attitude we bring to this intimate exchange: whether our prayers are heartfelt rather than just a mental exercise. It is always through the heart that our prayers are heard, even if we first make the connection in our feet or hands. Do we really feel the suffering of the earth, sense its need? Do we feel this connection with creation, do we feel ourselves a part of this beautiful and suffering being? Then our prayers are alive, a living stream that flows from our heart. Then every step, every touch, will be a prayer for the earth, a remembrance of what is sacred. We are a part of the earth calling to its Creator, crying in its time of need.[98]

7

PERSONAL PRAYER

"Every being knows its own way of prayer and praise,"[99] and part of the inner journey is to discover and then live this prayer. My own journey has taken me to the prayer of the heart—a prayer born of need and longing, an opening to the mystery of love that is always present within. It is a deep prayer of silence and love in which the heart looks towards its Beloved. For this prayer of the heart there is no set time, nor any ritual, because it is the most intimate cry of the heart. Often in the night I lie awake feeling a sweet pain that turns me towards the One I love. Sometimes tears run down my face and my heart aches. I may try to put words to this prayer; sometimes the words flow with the tenderness with which lovers whisper to the one they love, and sometimes words come with anguish, when I feel so separate, so abandoned, left alone with the heart's longing. But deeper than any words is the silence that calls, a silence that I need and that mysteriously also needs me.

This is the primal prayer of my soul, a merging into the emptiness that is within, at the very center of my heart. Here there is a giving of myself to my Beloved with a totality that is a complete belonging to love. I feel that I am the very core of my longing, a desire that comes from the heart and embraces every breath, every cell of my body. All of my being and body is then in prayer, and nothing is excluded from this prayer, this turning of the heart, this pouring out of my whole self. Every cell of the body feels this sweet anguish, the potency of this prayer of love. And I wait, hoping, longing, needing my Beloved more than I know. And then, when I feel my Beloved, feel that love present within, I come to know the essence of prayer, that there is no separation, that we are always together in love. This is the mystery of oneness.

There came the time when this prayer became continuous, a prayer without ceasing—because how can the heart forget its Beloved, how can it not look towards the Source of its love and longing? As I have mentioned, this awakening within the heart, this birth of continual prayer, is one of the miracles of the path. Whatever moment of the day, whatever outer activities, when I look within I see this mystery that is praying, and I experience the silence and wonder of how the heart is a place of prayer, an altar of love. I feel the tenderness, the sweetness, the power of this prayer. This prayer is the essence of my being, a covenant of love, a remembrance, a meeting and a merging. It is a living oneness within me that belongs to every moment of the day and night.[100] This prayer is my practice, an offering of my self, my own most intimate way of being with my Beloved. What else can I do in this world but pray? We are love's prayer.

NOTES

OPENING PAGES

1. Theophanis the Monk, a monastic of the Christian East. Quoted by James Cutsinger, "The Ladder of Divine Ascent," *Merton and Hesychasm*, p. 76.
2. Quoted by al-Qushayrī, *Principles of Sufism*, trans. B.R.von Schlegell, p. 275-6.

INTRODUCTION

3. I use the term "God" not in reference to an anthropomorphic father-figure, or other personified image, but to an all-pervading, ever-present Reality that is both immanent ("closer to him than his neck vein," Qur'an 50:16) and transcendent ("beyond even our idea of the beyond"). Sufis call this Reality the "Beloved."
4. *Interior Castle*, trans. Mirabai Starr, Introduction, p. 11.
5. Ibid., p. 12.
6. *For Lovers of God Everywhere: Poems of the Christian Mystics*, by Roger Housden, p. 90.
7. Quoted by Kallistos Ware, *Merton and Hesychasm*, p. 6.
8. For a detailed description of the chambers of the heart in the Sufi tradition, see Vaughan-Lee, *Fragments of a Love Story: Reflections on the Life of a Mystic*, chap. 1, "Chambers of the Heart."
9. Theophan the Recluse calls the prayer of feeling the "third degree of prayer," after prayer of the body and prayer of the mind. *The Art of Prayer*, p. 52.
10. *Interior Castle*, trans. E. Allison Peers, Seventh Mansion, chap. 3, p. 222.

1. PRAYER AND LISTENING

11. In the Sufi tradition, if one is to pray for another it is best if there is a personal connection or link. Then one just needs to say within the heart the first name of this person, offering it to God, and then let the thought go. One can also place the person within one's heart.

12. *Life of St. Teresa*, chap. XV.

13. *Newsweek*, January 6, 1992, "Talking to God," p. 44.

14. Trans. Andrew Harvey, *Light Upon Light*, p. 99.

15. Molinos, Miguel, "Spiritual Guide," quoted by Evelyn Underhill, *Mysticism*, p. 324. Molinos (d. 1697) was the chief apostle of Quietism, which had an indirect effect on St. Teresa of Avila. St. Teresa also says that as we begin to sense that God hears our prayers, we should remain inwardly silent: "When from the secret signs He gives us we seem to realize that He is hearing us, it is well for us to keep silence." *Interior Castle*, Fourth Mansion, chap. 3, p. 88. Quietism was finally condemned by the church in 1687, Molinos was imprisoned for life in the same year.

16. *Interior Castle*, trans. E. Allison Peers, Sixth Mansion, chap. 3, p. 138.

17. Ibid., p. 139.

18. Ibid., pp. 142-3.

19. Ibid., pp. 145-6.

20. "Hearing voices" is a well-known expression of schizophrenia, and the mystic quickly learns when and when not to tell others about their inner voice.

21. St. Teresa expresses the importance of humility in prayer, "the whole foundation of prayer must be laid in humility." *The Autobiography of St.Teresa of Avila*, chap. 12, p. 192.

22. The mystical journey is sometimes referred to as "the journey from the alone to the Alone."

23. *Interior Castle*, trans. E. Allison Peers, Seventh Mansion, chap. 1, p. 210.

2. STAGES OF PRAYER

24. *Interior Castle*, trans. E. Allison Peers, First Mansion, chap. 1.
25. Gerard Manley Hopkins, "I wake and feel the fell of dark not day.", lines 6-8, *The Poems and Prose of Gerard Manley Hopkins*.
26. Irina Tweedie, *Daughter of Fire*, p. 404.
27. *The Autobiography of St. Teresa of Avila*, chap. 11, p. 82.
28. *The Conference of the Birds*, trans. C. S. Nott, p. 33.
29. *I Corinthians* 13:7.
30. *The Autobiography of St. Teresa of Avila*, chap. 11, p. 83.
31. Irina Tweedie, *Daughter of Fire*, p. 79. St. Teresa describes the Prayer of Quiet as "a little spark of True Love that the Lord begins to ignite in the soul." *Teresa of Avila: The Book of My Life*, trans. Mirabai Starr, p. 103.
32. Hopkins, "No worst there is none. Pitched past pitch of grief.", lines 3-4, *The Poems and Prose of Gerard Manley Hopkins*.
33. Sanā'i, quoted by Javad Nurbakhsh, *Sufi Symbolism: Volume II*, p. 121.
34. Quoted by Annemarie Schimmel, *Mystical Dimensions of Islam*, p. 72.
35. *The Autobiography of St. Teresa of Avila*, chap. 14, pp. 107-9.
36. Ibid., p. 107.
37. *Interior Castle*, trans. E. Allison Peers, Fifth Mansion, chap. 1, p. 103.
38. *Song of Solomon* 5:5-6.
39. *Interior Castle*, trans. E. Allison Peers, Fifth Mansion, chap. 2, p. 109.
40. Jeanne Guyon, *The Song of the Bride*, p. 110.
41. *The Autobiography of St. Teresa of Avila*, chap. 17, p. 135.
42. *Interior Castle*, trans. E. Allison Peers, Fifth Mansion, chap. 2, p. 109.
43. *Sūra* 24:37.
44. This practice of inner seclusion belongs especially to the Naqshbandi Sufi order and their principle of "Solitude in the Crowd." In the words of Sa'īd al-Kharrāz, "Perfection is not in exhibitions of miraculous powers, but perfection is to sit among

people, sell and buy, marry and have children; and yet never leave the presence of Allāh even for one moment."

45. Quoted by James Arraj, *St. John of the Cross and Dr. C. G. Jung*, p. 60.

46. Sermon, "Blessed are the Poor."

47. *The Autobiography of St. Teresa of Avila*, chap. 18, p. 147.

48. Ibid., chap. 18, p. 146. 'Attār describes a similar mystical state: "I know nothing, I understand nothing. I am unaware of myself. I am in love, but with whom I am in love I do not know. My heart is at the same time both full and empty of love." *The Conference of the Birds*, p. 119.

49. 'Attār, *The Conference of the Birds*, trans. C. S. Nott, p. 122.

50. Quoted by Schimmel, *I Am Wind, You Are Fire*, p. 172.

51. *The Cloud of Unknowing*, chap. 8, quoted by Happold, *Mysticism: A Study and an Anthology*, p. 312.

3. THE JESUS PRAYER AND THE DHIKR

52. The Jesus Prayer originated with the early Desert Fathers in Egypt in the fifth century. It is first mentioned by St. Diadochos of Photiki, in the first volume of *The Philokalia*.

53. Naqshbandis are known as the Silent Sufis because their spiritual practices are in silence. Bahā ad-Dīn Naqshband (d. 1389), after whom this order is named, taught that God is most easily reached in silence.

54. Traditional Sufi prayer beads are 99, echoing the 99 Names of God. An Orthodox prayer rope has 100 knots.

55. Quoted by R. A. Nicholson, *Studies in Islamic Mysticism*, p. 7.

56. Abd al-Qādir al-Jīlānī, *The Secret of Secrets*, trans. Tosun Bayrak, p. 45.

57. Kallistos Ware, "The Power of the Name," *Merton and Hesychasm*, p. 58.

58. Ibid., pp. 58-9.

59. *The Way of A Pilgrim*, p. 14.

60. In *I Thessalonians* 5:17 the Apostle Paul tells believers to "Pray without ceasing."

61. Schimmel, *Mystical Dimensions of Islam*, p. 169.

62. Kallistos Ware, *Merton and Hesychasm*, p. 58.

63. *The Art of Prayer*, p. 97.

64. *Judges* 13:18.

65. *St. John* 16:23. Quoted by Kallistos Ware, *Merton and Hesychasm*, p. 51.

66. Kallistos Ware, *Merton and Hesychasm*, p. 62.

67. *The Art of Prayer*, p. 36.

68. The cycle of the breath thus begins with the out-breath. Other Sufi *dhikrs*, such as "*Lā ilāha illā 'llāh*," also begin with the out-breath—"with each exhalation of his breath, he says, '*Lā ilāha*,' and with each inhalation, '*illā 'llāh*.'" In both the Christian Orthodox tradition and Sufism there are also more elaborate techniques with the breath, including slowing the breath, synchronizing it with the beatings of the heart, and moving the breath to different parts of the body. However, it is advised that one needs a teacher for these more advanced breathing practices.

69. Bahā ad-Dīn Naqshband, from the first of the Eleven Naqshbandi Principles.

70. The final teaching of Irina Tweedie's Naqshbandi sheikh was: "There is nothing but Nothingness." *Daughter of Fire*, p. 729.

71. With the "Allāh hu" *dhikr* which is chanted out loud at group *dhikrs* in Turkey and Central Asia, "(Al)lāh" is recited on the in-breath and "hu" (which can be interpreted as the article) is very forcibly chanted on the out-breath. So with the word "Allāh" the soul returns to its spiritual home.

72. Interestingly other Sufi teachings describe the reverse, that the in-breath brings us into the world of creation and the out-breath returns us to the Source:

> The rhythm to which the breathing is subjected is the rhythm of creation and dissolution, of Beauty and Majesty. Breathing in represents creation, that is, the Outward Manifestation of the Divine Qualities, the flowing of the ink from the *Alif* into the *Bā* and the other letters of the alphabet; breathing out represents the return of the Qualities to the Essence; the next intake of breath is a new creation, and so on. The final expiring [i.e. the last

out-breath of someone at the point of death] symbolizes the realization of the Immutability which underlies the illusory vicissitudes of creation and dissolution, the realization of the truth that God was and there was naught else beside Him. He is now even as He was.

Quoted by Martin Lings, *A Sufi Saint of the Twentieth Century*, p. 159.

73. To quote a Naqshbandi description of the *dhikr*: "we begin on the out-breath with *al*, to 'empty ourselves of ourselves,' and we continue on the in-breath with *lāh*, to 'fill ourselves with His Presence.'"

74. *The Way of A Pilgrim*, p. 30.

75. Quoted by Schimmel, *Mystical Dimensions of Islam*, p. 46.

4. THE CIRCLE OF LOVE

76. Rūmī, trans. Andrew Harvey, *Love's Fire: Recreations of Rumi*, p. 77.

77. For the Sufi the lament of the *ney*, the reed flute, evokes this primal cry of separation, as expressed at the beginning of Rūmī's *Mathnawī*:

> Listen to the reed how it tells a tale, complaining
>   of separations,
> Saying, "Ever since I was parted from the reed-bed,
>   my lament has caused man and woman to moan.
> It is only to a bosom torn by severance that I can unfold
>   the pain of love-desire.
> Everyone who is left far from his source wishes back the
>   time when he was united with it."

78. Annemarie Schimmel, *Mystical Dimensions of Islam*, p. 148.

79. Ibid., p. 150.

80. Rūmī, *Mathnawī*, quoted by R. A. Nicholson, *The Mystics of Islam*, p. 113.

81. Quoted by al-Qushayrī, *Principles of Sufism*, p. 278.
82. *The Cloud of Unknowing*, quoted by T.S. Eliot, "Little Gidding," line 238.
83. Quoted by al-Qushayrī, *Principles of Sufism*, p. 282.
84. Quoted by Claude Addas, *Quest for the Red Sulphur: The Life of Ibn 'Arabī*, p. 61.
85. Quoted by Schimmel, *Mystical Dimensions of Islam*, p. 165.

5. THE HEART PRAYS

86. *The Enlightened Heart*, ed. Stephen Mitchell, p. 89.
87. Trans. William Chittick, *The Sufi Path of Love*, p. 241.
88. Anonymous Sufi saying.
89. Nizāmī, *The Story of Layla and Majnun*, trans. R. Gelpke, p. 195.
90. The Sufi says that there are three journeys, "The Journey from God," (when we forget our divine nature and become immersed in the attractions of the world), "The Journey to God," (the return journey, *fanā*, the annihilation of the ego), and "The Journey in God," (*baqā*, abiding in God).
91. Theophan the Recluse describes how when prayer becomes continuous "the spiritual prayer may be said to begin. This is the gift of the Holy Spirit praying for us, the last degree of prayer which our minds can grasp." *The Art of Prayer*, p. 52.
92. In the Orthodox tradition, the prayer of the heart becomes "the incarnation of Jesus in the heart, in which the remembrance of God becomes the ceaseless Presence of Christ in the heart." Vincent Rossi, "Presence, Participation, Performance: The Remembrance of God in the Early Hesychast Fathers," *Paths to the Heart: Sufism and the Christian East*, ed. James Cutsinger, p. 107.
93. *Interior Castle*, trans. E. Allison Peers, Seventh Mansion, chap. 4, p. 229.
94. For the Sufi this world is a place of divine revelation; "I was a hidden treasure and I longed to be known, so I created the world."

6. PRAYER FOR THE EARTH

95. "God taught Adam the names, all of them." (Qur'an 2:31) In the Bible it is stated that "Adam gave names to all cattle, and to the fowl of the air, and to every beast of the field." (*Genesis* 2:20) Adam in Hebrew means "human being."

96. The Qur'an explains that humanity holds a privileged position among God's creations on earth: we are chosen as *khalifa*, "vice-regent" and carry the responsibility of caring for God's earthly creations. "'Behold,' Thy Lord said to the angels, 'I will create a vice-regent on earth.'" (*Sūra* 2:30)

97. Carl Jung describes the tragedy that "man himself has ceased to be the microcosm and his anima is no longer the consubstantial *scintilla* or spark of the *anima mundi*, the World Soul." *Collected Works*, vol. 11, p. 759.

98. For more material on the need for a spiritual response to our present ecological crisis, see www.workingwithoneness.org/spiritual-ecology.

7. PERSONAL PRAYER

99. "Do you not see that all that is in the heavens and the earth, and the bird in its flying, is praising Allāh? For every being knows its own way of prayer and praise; and Allāh is the Knower of all that they do." (Qur'an 21:41)

100. For more on the author's own personal spiritual journey, see *Fragments of a Love Story: Reflections on the Life of a Mystic*.

INDEX

BIBLIOGRAPHY

Addas, Claude. *Quest for the Red Sulphur: The Life of Ibn 'Arabī.* Cambridge: The Islamic Texts Society, 1994.

Arraj, James. *St. John of the Cross and Dr. C. G. Jung.* Chiloquin, Oregon: Inner Growth Books, 1986.

'Attār, Farīd ud-Dīn. *The Conference of the Birds.* Trans. C. S. Nott. London: Routledge & Kegan Paul, 1961.

The Bible, Authorized Version. London: 1611.

Chariton, Igumen of Valamo. *The Art of Prayer.* Trans. E. Kadloubovsky and E. M. Palmer. London: Faber & Faber, 1966.

Chittick, William C. *The Sufi Path of Love.* Albany: State University of New York Press, 1983.

Cutsinger, James, S., Ed. *Paths to the Heart: Sufism and the Christian East.* Bloomington, Indiana: World Wisdom, 2002.

Diker, Bernadette & Mintaldo, Jonathan, Ed. *Merton and Hesychasm.* Louisville, Kentucky: Fons Vitae, 2003.

Eliot, T. S. *Collected Poems.* London: Faber and Faber, 1963.

French, R. M., Trans. *The Way of A Pilgrim.* New York: Harper Collins, 1965.

Guyon, Jeanne. *The Song of the Bride.* Auburn, Maine: The Seed Sowers, 1990.

Harvey, Andrew. *Light Upon Light.* Berkeley: North Atlantic Books, 1996.

Hopkins, Gerard Manley. *The Poems and Prose of Gerard Manley Hopkins.* Harmondsworth: Penguin Books, 1953.

Housden, Roger. *For Lovers of God Everywhere: Poems of the Christian Mystics.* Carlsbad, California: Hay House, 2009.

Jīlānī, 'Abd al-Qādir al-. *The Secret of Secrets.* Trans. Shaykh Tosun Bayrak. Cambridge: The Islamic Texts Society, 1992.

Jung, C. G. *Collected Works.* London: Routledge & Kegan Paul.

Qur'an. Trans. Muhammad Asad. Bristol: Book Foundation, 2003.

Qushayrī, al-. *Principles of Sufism.* Trans. B. R. von Schlegell. Berkeley: Mizan Press, 1990.

Lings, Martin. *A Sufi Saint of the Twentieth Century: Shaikh Ahmad al-'Alawī.* Cambridge: Islamic Texts Society, 1993.

Mitchell, Stephen, Ed. *The Enlightened Heart*. New York: Harper & Row, 1989.

Nicholson, R. A. *Studies in Islamic Mysticism*. Cambridge: Cambridge University Press, 1921.

Nizāmī. *The Story of Layla and Majnun*. Trans. R. Gelpke. London: Bruno Cassirer, 1966.

Nurbakhsh, Javad. *Sufi Symbolism: Volume II*. London: Khaniqahi-Nimatullahi Publications, 1987.

Rūmī. *Love's Fire: Recreations of Rumi*. Trans. Andrew Harvey. Ithaca, New York: Meerama, 1989.

Schimmel, Annemarie. *Mystical Dimensions of Islam*. Chapel Hill: University of North Carolina Press, 1975.

—. *I Am Wind, You Are Fire*. Boston: Shambhala Publications, 1992.

Teresa of Avila. *Interior Castle*. Trans. E. Allison Peers. New York: Doubleday, 1961.

—. *Interior Castle*. Trans. Mirabai Starr. New York: Riverhead Books, 2003.

—. *The Autobiography of St. Teresa of Avila: The Life of St. Teresa of Jesus*. Trans. David Lewis. Charlotte, North Carolina: Tan Books, 2010.

—. *Teresa of Avila: The Book of My Life*. Trans. Mirabai Starr. Boston: Shambhala, 2007.

Tweedie, Irina. *Daughter of Fire: A Diary of a Spiritual Training with a Sufi Master*. Point Reyes, California: The Golden Sufi Center, 1986.

Underhill, Evelyn. *Mysticism*. New York: New American Library, 1974.

Vaughan-Lee, Llewellyn. *Fragments of a Love Story: Reflections on the Life of a Mystic*. Point Reyes, California: The Golden Sufi Center, 2011.

ACKNOWLEDGMENTS

For permission to use copyrighted material, the author gratefully wishes to acknowledge: selections from *Mystical Dimensions of Islam* by Annemarie Schimmel, copyright ©1975 by the Univ. of North Carolina Press, www.uncpress.unc.edu; Fons Vitae for permission to quote from *Merton and Hesychasm*, editors Bernadette Diker and Jonathan Mintaldo, copyright ©2003, www.fonsvitae.com.

ABOUT THE AUTHOR

LLEWELLYN VAUGHAN-LEE, Ph.D., is a Sufi teacher in the Naqshbandiyya-Mujaddidiyya Sufi Order. Born in London in 1953, he has followed the Naqshbandi Sufi path since he was nineteen. In 1991 he became the successor of Irina Tweedie, author of *Daughter of Fire: A Diary of a Spiritual Training with a Sufi Master*. He then moved to Northern California and founded The Golden Sufi Center (www.goldensufi.org). Author of several books, he has specialized in the area of dreamwork, integrating the ancient Sufi approach to dreams with the insights of Jungian Psychology. Since 2000 the focus of his writing and teaching has been on spiritual responsibility in our present time of transition, and an awakening global consciousness of oneness. More recently he has written about the feminine, the *anima mundi* (world soul), and spiritual ecology (see www.workingwithoneness.org).

THE GOLDEN SUFI CENTER® PUBLICATIONS
www.goldensufi.org/books.html

LOVE IS A FIRE:
The Sufi's Mystical Journey Home

THE CIRCLE OF LOVE

CATCHING THE THREAD:
Sufism, Dreamwork, and Jungian Psychology

THE FACE BEFORE I WAS BORN:
A Spiritual Autobiography

THE PARADOXES OF LOVE

SUFISM, THE TRANSFORMATION OF THE HEART

IN THE COMPANY OF FRIENDS:
Dreamwork within a Sufi Group

THE BOND WITH THE BELOVED:
The Mystical Relationship of the Lover and the Beloved

⌒

EDITED *by* LLEWELLYN VAUGHAN-LEE
with biographical information by SARA SVIRI

TRAVELLING THE PATH OF LOVE:
Sayings of Sufi Masters

⌒

ABOUT THE PUBLISHER

THE GOLDEN SUFI CENTER publishes books, video, and audio on Sufism and mysticism. A California religious nonprofit 501 (c) (3) corporation, it is dedicated to making the teachings of the Naqshbandi Sufi path available to all seekers. For further information about activities and publications, please contact:

THE GOLDEN SUFI CENTER
P.O. Box 456
Point Reyes Station, CA 94956-0456
tel: 415-663-0100 · fax: 415-663-0103
www.goldensufi.org